AAT L3
Advanced Book-keeping

(AAT Exam Practice Assessments)

Contents	Page
Mock Exam One	5
Solutions to Mock Exam One	21
Mock Exam Two	41
Solutions to Mock Exam Two	57
Mock Exam Three	79
Solutions to Mock Exam Three	95
Mock Exam Four	117
Solutions to Mock Exam Four	135
Mock Exam Five	157
Solutions to Mock Exam Five	175

This book consists of FIVE 'real style' AAT Exam Practice Assessments to give you lots of exam practice and the very best chance of exam success.

We also sell Study Text and Exam Practice Kits produced by our expert team of AAT tutors. Our team have extensive experience teaching AAT and writing high quality study materials that enable you to focus and pass your exam. Our Study Text and Exam Practice Kits cover all aspects of the syllabus in a user friendly way and build on your understanding by including real style exam activities for you to practice.

Visit www.acornlive.com/aat-home-study/ for further information.

Our AAT tutors work very long hours to produce study material that is first class and absolutely focused on passing your exam. We hope very much that you enjoy this product and wish you the very best for exam success! For feedback please contact our team aatlivelearning@gmail.com or safina@acornlive.com

Polite Notice! © Distributing our digital materials such as uploading and sharing them on social media or e-mailing them to your friends is copyright infringement.

Mock Exam One
AAT L3 Advanced Book-keeping

Assessment information:

You have **2 hours** to complete this practice assessment.

This assessment contains **5 tasks** and you should attempt to complete **every** task.
Each task is independent. You will not need to refer to your answers to previous tasks.
Read every task carefully to make sure you understand what is required.

The standard rate of VAT is 20%.

Where the date is relevant, it is given in the task data.
Both minus signs and brackets can be used to indicate negative numbers **unless** task instructions say otherwise.

You must use a full stop to indicate a decimal point. For example, write 100.57 not 100,57 or 100 57

You may use a comma to indicate a number in the thousands, but you don't have to. For example, 10000 and 10,000 are both acceptable.

Task 1 (21 marks)

This task is about non-current assets.

You are working on the accounting records of a business known as A.N. Business.

A.N. Business is a VAT registered business.

The business has part-exchanged an item of machinery in its factory. The following is the relevant purchase invoice for the new machine.

To: A.N. Business	From: Z Business Invoice number: 1123	Date: 1 Sept 20X6
Item	**Details**	**£**
Machine AZ50	AZ50	19,000.00
Software	for AZ50	1,290.00
2 x PC Monitors (screens)	@ £150 each for AZ50	300.00
Delivery and installation	for AZ50	800.00
Net total		21,390.00
VAT 20%		4,278.00
Total		25,668.00

VAT can be reclaimed on the purchase of these items.

The following relates to the machine replaced by the business.

Item description	Machine AX56
Date of purchase	01/09/X4
Date of sale	24/07/X7
Part-exchange value	£2,000.00 plus VAT

- A.N. Business has a policy of capitalising expenditure over £200.
- Plant and machinery is depreciated at 25% per annum on a diminishing balance basis.
- Motor vehicles are depreciated at 35% per annum on a diminishing balance basis.
- A full year's depreciation is charged in the year of acquisition and none in the year of disposal.

(a) For the year ended 31 August 20X7, record the following in the extract from the non-current asset register below.

- Any acquisitions of non-current assets
- Any disposals of non-current assets
- Depreciation

(18 marks)

Note: Not every cell will require an entry and not all cells will accept entries.
Choose answers where a grey picklist is required and insert numerical answers in the highlighted grey cells only.
Show your numerical answers to TWO decimal places.
Use DD/MM/YY format for any dates.

Description /Serial number	Acquisition date	Cost £	Depreciation charges £	Carrying amount £	Funding method	Disposal proceeds £	Disposal date
Plant and machinery							
Machine AX56	01/09/X4	13000.00			Loan		
Year ended 31/08/X5			3250.00	9750.00			
Year ended 31/08/X6			2437.50	7312.50			
Year ended 31/08/X7			Picklist 1	Picklist 2			
Picklist 3					Picklist 4		
Year ended 31/08/X7							
Motor vehicles							
Car EN65 RBV	23/01/X6	6700.00			Loan		
Year ended 31/08/X6			2345.00	4355.00			
Year ended 31/08/X7							
Car BN60 DFV	26/08/X5	7800.00			Finance lease		
Year ended 31/08/X5			2730.00	5070.00			
Year ended 31/08/X6			1774.50	3295.50			
Year ended 31/08/X7							

Picklist 1	Picklist 2	Picklist 3	Picklist 4
0.00	9750.00	Machine AX56	Cash
2031.25	7312.50	Car BN60 DFV	Lease arrangement
1828.13	0.00	Car EN65 RBV	Hire Purchase
1523.44	13000.00	Machine AZ50	Part Exchange

(b) Complete the following calculation (3 marks)

Calculate the gain or loss on disposal of Machine AX56 for the year ended 31 August 20X7. **Show your answer rounded to TWO decimal places. Use a minus sign or brackets to indicate a loss on disposal.**

£ [   ]

End of Task

Task 2 (17 marks)

This task is about ledger accounting for non-current assets.

You are working on the accounting records of a business for the year ended 31 August 20X7.

VAT can be ignored.

A new machine has been acquired, the cost was £18,930 and the purchase was paid for from the business bank account. The business plans to sell the new machine after 5 years when its residual value is expected to be £2,000.

Machines are depreciated using the straight-line method. A full year's depreciation is charged in the year of acquisition. Depreciation has already been entered in the accounting records of the business for existing machines and the amount is shown below in the ledger accounts.

Make entries in the ledger accounts below for the acquisition and depreciation charge for the new machine for the year ended 31 August 20X7. For each ledger account show clearly the balance to be carried down or transferred to the statement of profit or loss, as appropriate.

(a) Calculate the depreciation charge of the new machine for the year ended 31 August 20X7

£ [   ]

Make entries in the accounts below for:

- **The acquisition of the new machine**
- **The depreciation charge for the new machine**

(12 marks)

Picklist: Bank, Depreciation charges, Disposals, Machinery accumulated depreciation, Machinery at cost, Profit or loss account, Purchases, Purchases ledger control account, Sales, Sales ledger control account, Machine running expenses. Balance b/d, Balance c/d.

Machinery at cost

	£			£
Balance b/d	84900		⇕	
⇕			⇕	
⇕			⇕	
	84900			0

Machinery accumulated depreciation

	£			£
⇕		Balance b/d		49200
⇕			⇕	
⇕			⇕	
	0			49200

Depreciation charges

	£			£
Balance b/d	22600		⇕	
⇕			⇕	
⇕			⇕	
	22600			0

A business sold a van during its accounting period. The van originally cost £18,000 and had accumulated depreciation of £12,600. It was sold for £1,600 and the money was deposited in the business bank account. The accounting policy of the business is that no depreciation is charged in the year of disposal.

(b) Drag and drop the account names to the debit and credit columns to show the accounting entries for the £1,600 proceeds received from sale of the van.

(2 marks)

Disposals

Debit

Credit

Motor vehicles at cost

Bank

(c) Complete the following sentence. Do NOT use brackets or a minus sign.

(3 marks)

The business made a (**Picklist:** Gain, Loss) on the disposal of the van of £ [   ]

End of Task

Task 3 (19 marks)

This task is about ledger accounting, including accruals and prepayments.

You are working on the accounting records of a business for the year ended 31 December 20X7.

In this task you are to ignore VAT.

Business policy: accounting for accruals and prepayments
An entry is made to the income or expense account and an opposite entry to the relevant asset or liability account. In the following period, asset or liability entries are reversed.

You are looking at motor vehicle expenses for the year.

- The cash book for the year shows payments for motor vehicle expenses of £8,042.
- This includes £1,467 for the following payments relating to vehicle insurance.

Insurance Car EN15 RBV	**Insurance Car SG67 EEF**
Insurance for the period 1 May 20X7 to 30 April 20X8. **£900 for the period.**	Insurance for the period 1 January 20X7 to 31 December 20X7. **£567 for the period.**

(a) Complete the following statement. Do NOT use a minus sign or brackets.

(4 marks)

The motor vehicle expense account needs an adjustment for

[_____⬇] of £ [_____] dated [_____⬇]

Picklist	**Picklist**
Accrued expenses	31/12/X8
Accrued income	31/12/X7
Prepaid expenses	30/04/X8
Prepaid income	01/01/X7

(b) Update the motor vehicle expenses account

Show clearly:

- the cash book figure
- the year end adjustment
- the transfer to the statement of profit or loss for the year.   (6 marks)

Motor vehicle expenses

		£			£
	⇅			⇅	
	⇅			⇅	
	⇅			⇅	
		0			0

Picklist: Motor vehicle expenses, Bank, Accrued expenses, Accrued income, Accrued income (reversal), Accrued expenses (reversal), Prepaid income, Statement of financial position, Prepaid income (reversal), Prepaid expenses (reversal), Profit or loss account, Prepaid expenses, Purchases ledger control account, Sales, Sales ledger control account, Balance b/d, Balance c/d.

(c) Enter the figures in the table shown below to the appropriate trial balance debit or credit columns.

Do not enter zeros in unused column cells. Do NOT use minus signs or brackets.

(2 marks)

Extract from the trial balance

Account	Ledger balance £	Trial balance £ DR	Trial balance £CR
Prepaid income	1000		
Drawings	8900		
Carriage inwards	1029		
Accrued income	1504		

You are now reviewing interest received for the year ended 31 December 20X7.

- The business had accrued income for bank interest received of £45 at the beginning of the accounting period.
- The cash book for the year shows receipts for bank interest received of £142.
- The £142 does not include £26 interest received which relates to the period 01/12/X7 to 31/12/X7, this was credited in the bank statements on 2 January 20X8.

(d) Calculate bank interest received that will be shown as income in the statement of profit or loss for the year ended 31 December 20X7. Complete the table shown below. If necessary, use a minus sign only to indicate any deductions from the cash book figure.

(4 marks)

	£
Cash book figure	
Opening adjustment	
Closing adjustment	
Bank interest received for the year ended 31/12/X7	

(e) Show whether the following statements are true or false.

(3 marks)

	TRUE	FALSE
Accrued income provided at the year end will have the effect of increasing profits within the statement of profit or loss for the year.	☐	☐
Prepaid income is a current asset included within the statement of financial position.	☐	☐
Accrued expenses are a current liability included within the statement of financial position.	☐	☐

End of Task

Task 4 (23 marks)

This task is about accounting adjustments.

You are a trainee accountant technician and work in a finance department.

A trial balance shown below has been drawn up and balanced using a suspense account. You now need to make some corrections and adjustments for the year ended 31 December 20X7.

You may ignore VAT in this task.

The allowance for doubtful debts needs to be adjusted to 2% of outstanding trade receivables.

(a) Refer to the extract from the extended trial balance below. Calculate the value of the adjustment required (to the nearest £).

(2 marks)

£ [   ]

(b) Record the adjustment in (a) and the following adjustments in the extract from the extended trial balance below.

(14 marks)

- Office expenses of £90 have been correctly posted to the cashbook but no corresponding debit entry was made to office expenses.
- The purchase ledger control account in the general ledger has been extracted and included in the trial balance incorrectly as £5,999. The correct balance should be £6,739.
- Staff wages of £1,080 were posted in error to office expenses.

Extract from the extended trial balance

Ledger account	Ledger balances		Adjustments	
	Dr £	Cr £	Dr £	Cr £
Bank	21932			
Opening inventory	6781			
Irrecoverable debts	750			
Capital		24976		
Office expenses	4200			
Staff wages	16339			
Allowance for doubtful debts		400		
Allowance for doubtful debts - adjustment				
Depreciation charges	2952			
Van at cost	17400			
Van accumulated depreciation		6090		
Purchases	45688			
Purchase ledger control account		5999		
Sales		79991		
Sales ledger control account	24090			
Suspense		650		

(c) Show the journal entries that will be required to close off the purchase ledger control account for the year ended 31 December 20X7 and select an appropriate narrative.

(4 marks)

Journal

Account	Dr £	Cr £
⬇		
⬇		

Narrative for journal

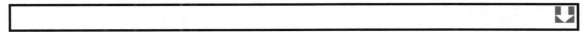

Picklist for journal: Van expenses, Bank, Statement of financial position, Profit or loss account, Purchases ledger control account, Purchases, Sales, Sales ledger control account, Balance b/d, Balance c/d.

Picklist for narrative: Transfer to the profit or loss account, Transfer to the statement of financial position, Closure of purchase ledger control account for the year ended 31 December 20X7, Transfer to a suspense account.

(d) Show the journal entries that will be required to adjust for closing inventory of £13,422 for the year ended 31 December 20X7.

(3 marks)

Account	Dr £	Cr £
⬇		
⬇		

Picklist: Bank, Closing inventory (statement of profit or loss account), Purchases ledger control account, Purchases, Sales, Sales ledger control account, Balance b/d, Balance c/d, Closing inventory (statement of financial position).

End of Task

Task 5 (20 marks)

This task is about period end routines, using accounting records, ethical principles and the extended trial balance.

You are preparing a purchases ledger control account reconciliation for a sole trader as at 31 May 20X7.

The current balance showing in the purchases ledger control account is a credit of £27,042 and the total in the purchases ledger for all supplier account balances are a credit balance of £22,044.

The purchases ledger has been compared to the purchases ledger control account and the following errors or omissions have been identified:

1.	The total column of the purchase daybook was undercast by £1,000. The amount posted to the purchase ledger control account was £131,673 and the correct amount should be £132,673.
2.	Purchase returns of £5,640 have been credited to the purchase ledger control account in error. The correct entries have been made in the purchases ledger accounts of suppliers.
3.	A purchase invoice of £240 from Streets Ltd was omitted from purchases daybook. The correct entry was made in the purchase ledger account of the supplier.
4.	A set-off entry of £5,042 was omitted from the purchase ledger account of M. Smith. The correct entry was made in purchases ledger control account.
5.	Purchase returns of £120 was debited in error to the purchase ledger account of Winkle Traders Ltd instead of the purchase ledger account of Traders RUS Ltd.
6.	A purchase invoice was sent by a supplier for £360 in error, the correct amount should have been £3,600. The incorrect amount of £360 was posted to both the purchases ledger and purchases ledger control account.

(a) Using the table below show THREE adjustments that should appear in the purchases ledger control account. Enter only ONE figure for each line. Do not enter zeros in unused cells. Do NOT use minus signs or brackets.

(6 marks)

Account	Dr £	Cr £
⬇		
⬇		
⬇		

Picklist: Adjustment 1, Adjustment 2, Adjustment 3, Adjustment 4, Adjustment 5, Adjustment 6

A colleague at work has raised a VAT matter and is concerned with how a certain VAT transaction should be treated in the accounting books and the VAT return of the business. The colleague asks Burt who is an AAT student but Burt knows little about VAT matters and is certainly not an expert.

(b) Which one of the following fundamental ethical principles would Burt most likely be in breach of, if he advised the colleague how the VAT matter should be dealt with.

(3 marks)

Integrity	☐
Professional competence and due care	☐
Confidentiality	☐

You are now working on the accounting records of a different business.

An extended trial balance is shown below and the adjustments have already been correctly entered.

(c) Extend the figures into the columns for the statement of profit or loss and the statement of financial position. Do NOT enter zeros into unused column cells. Complete the extended trial balance by totalling the columns and entering any profit or loss figure for the year ended.

(11 marks)

Extended trial balance

Ledger account	Ledger balances		Adjustments		Statement of profit or loss		Statement of financial position	
	Dr £	Cr £	Dr £	Cr £	Dr £	Cr £	Dr £	Cr £
Purchases	13870			1200				
Purchase ledger control account		4520	2300					
Sales		80242						
Sales ledger control account	13298			2300				
Staff wages	27581			6000				
Bank	40211			56				
Allowance for doubtful debts: adjustment			450					
Allowance for doubtful debts		1846		450				
Purchases returns		740						
Office expenses	5698		56					
Closing inventory			1042	1042				
Depreciation charges			4000					
Office equipment at cost	20000							
Office equipment accumulated depreciation		12000		4000				
Opening inventory	930							
VAT		3241						
Capital		30999						
Drawings	12000		7200					
⬑⬏								
Total	133588	133588	15048	15048	0	0	0	0

⬑⬏ **Picklist**
Profit/loss for the year
Suspense
Balance b/d
Balance c/d
Gross profit/loss for the year

Mock Exam One - Solutions
AAT L3 Advanced Book-keeping

You may find the following tutor notes useful when answering exam practice tasks.

Elements of the financial statements

Five elements make up the general ledger accounts and financial statements of a business.

Assets

A resource controlled by the business as a result of past events and from which future economic benefits (money) are expected to flow to the business.

- Premises, machines, motor vehicles, office equipment or furniture and fittings.
- Inventory currently for resale.
- Trade receivables (money to be 'received') also called sales ledger control account.
- Accrued income.
- Prepaid expenses.
- Money in the bank.
- Cash in hand.

Liabilities

A present obligation of the business arising from past events, the settlement of which is expected to result in an outflow from the business.

- VAT owed to HMRC
- Wages owed to staff
- Bank loans and overdrafts
- Trade payables (money to be 'paid') also called purchases ledger control account.
- Prepaid income.
- Accrued expenses.

Capital

The residual interest (whatever is left) from the assets of the business after deducting all of its liabilities. Total assets less total liabilities is equal to capital (also called 'net assets') of the business. This balance represents what is owed and accumulated by the business to its owner. A separate account for drawings can also be maintained in the general ledger, drawings is money taken from the business by the owner and rather than reducing the owners capital account for the money taken, a drawings account is kept as a separate account because it provides more information.

Income

Money earned or received by the business from the sale of goods or services that is makes or sells (its trade), or from other investments or trade sources.

- Cash sales (sales not on credit).
- Credit sales (sales on credit).
- Rent received from ownership and rental of premises.
- Bank interest received.
- Discounts received (PPD) from paying credit suppliers early.
- Commission received.

Expenses

Costs incurred or paid for by the business in the normal course of trade in order to earn income. The cost of goods sold and other expenses must be matched with the sales revenues earned in the same period.

- Cash purchases (inventory purchases for resale and not on credit).
- Credit purchases (inventory purchases for resale and on credit).
- Rent payments (if the business is renting a property).
- Staff wages
- Motor vehicle running costs.
- Advertising.
- Depreciation such as wear and tear or loss of value to long-term assets such as machines or motor vehicles.
- Bank interest and charges.
- Discounts allowed (PPD) to credit customers who pay early.
- Accountancy and legal services.
- Irrecoverable debts expense.
- Increase (debit)/Decrease (credit) in allowances for doubtful debts.

Income and expenses are used to work out the amount of profit the business has generated. Any profits are owed to the owner of the business and increase the capital account of the owner.

DEAD CLIC

Don't get clouded in the double entry logic, ledgers are balances kept for the five elements of the financial statements and we are increasing or decreasing these balances according to the rules of double entry.

Important double entry terminology

DEAD CLIC defines what is the 'normal balance' or the natural state for a T account (general, sales or purchase ledger account).

DEAD CLIC is an acronym which gives the elements of financial statements and whether each element would be a debit or credit balance overall within a double entry ledger system. It can be used for determining the correct debit or credit balance but the element must be determined first. It can also be used to determine the correct double entry to increase or decrease an account balance.

DEAD CLIC

Debit	Credit
Expenses	Liabilities
Assets	Income
Drawings	Capital

The elements	Natural state	Increase balance (as per the natural state)	Decrease balance (opposite to natural state)
Income	Credit	Credit	Debit
Expenses	Debit	Debit	Credit
Assets	Debit	Debit	Credit
Liabilities	Credit	Credit	Debit
Capital	Credit	Credit	Debit

Totalling and balancing ledger accounts

1. Look at both sides of the ledger account and find the side which has the biggest total amount (debits or credits).
2. Add up the 'total' of all the entries on the side that has the biggest total amount and put this 'total' amount on both sides of the ledger account.
3. Add up all the entries on the side of the ledger account that had the smallest total amount.
4. Work out on the side that had the smallest total amount, the difference between the total amount entered and the other entries made on this side. This is the balance carried down (c/d) at the end of the period.
5. The balance c/d is entered on the side of the ledger account that had the smallest total amount to ensure that both total amounts entered on either side of the ledger account agrees. This as an arithmetical control and considered good practice in manual ledger accounting.

The balance c/d is only a balancing figure to ensure both sides of the ledger account agree at the end of the period. The true debit or credit balance is brought down (b/d) on the opposite side to the balance carried down (c/d). The balance b/d is on the 1st (beginning) of the month and the balance c/d is at the end of the month 30th/31st (ignoring February).

The trial balance and errors

The purpose of a trial balance is to ensure that all entries made in an organisation's general ledger are properly balanced and to check the accuracy of entries made before a final set of financial accounts are produced. If the totals for debit and credit balances do not agree then errors have definitely occurred, but even if the totals for debit and credit balances do agree it does not guarantee the general ledger balances are free from errors or omissions.

Types of errors not disclosed by the trial balance

The following types of error all have one thing in common, the same amount has been debited and credited within the general ledger, but an error has still occurred. These type of errors do not cause an imbalance when a trial balance is prepared (total debits equal total credits in the trial balance). Types of errors not disclosed by the trial balance can be remembered using the acronym 'TOPCROC'. Because the trial balance will still balance these types of error are more difficult to detect.

- **T Transposition** (two or more digits are reversed when amounts are entered).
- **O Original entry** (errors occur when documents such as invoices or credit notes are prepared incorrectly or when erroneous documents are posted to the day books).
- **P Principle** (mis posting to the WRONG ledger account and WRONG financial element), for example an 'expense' debited instead to an 'asset', a fundamental error because assets and profits will be under or overstated.
- **C Commission** (mis posting to the WRONG ledger account but RIGHT financial element), for example an 'expense' debited instead to another type of 'expense', less fundamental than an error of principle because assets and profits will be not be under or overstated.
- **R Reversal of entries** (the debit and credit mis posted the wrong way around).
- **O Omission** of a transaction (no posting made in the general ledger).
- **C Compensating** errors (very rare but this can happen), two independent errors for two different amounts posted as a debit and credit, the two errors compensate and cancel each other out. The trial balance will still balance.

Types of errors disclosed by the trial balance

The following types of error all have one thing in common, they all cause an imbalance when a trial balance is prepared (total debits do not equal total credits in the trial balance). Types of errors disclosed by the trial balance can be remembered using the acronym 'TESCOS'.

- **T Transposition** e.g. error posted incorrectly on one side of a ledger account but correctly posted on the other side such as debit expenses £54 and credit bank £45.
- **E Extraction** e.g. a ledger balance is not totalled and balanced correctly, so the wrong ledger balance is now 'extracted' and represented incorrectly in the trial balance.
- **S Single entry** e.g. a debit entry posted, but no credit entry posted, or vice versa.
- **C Casting** (casting means 'adding') e.g. a column in a day book casted (added up) incorrectly and the incorrect amount posted to the general ledger.
- **O Omission** of a ledger balance within the trial balance e.g. a ledger balance completely missed out and not included in the trial balance.
- **S Same sided** e.g. 2 debit entries only posted in error, or 2 credit entries only posted in error, rather than a debit and a credit entry made correctly.

Examples of how suspense accounts are opened

Example 1

Trial Balance (totals before suspense account opened)	154,896	155,279
Suspense account opened (debit balance)	383	
Trial balance totals agree until error(s) found	155,279	155,279

Example 1 the trial balance does not balance. The suspense account is always opened for the difference that exists between debits and credits and to ensure debits equal credits. The larger amount is credit £155,279 and the smaller amount is debit £154,896. A debit amount of £155,279 - £154,896 = £383 is missing. A suspense account is opened as £383 debit balance to ensure the trial balance agrees and until the error(s) has been found.

Example 2

Trial Balance (totals before suspense account opened)	121,780	99,800
Suspense account opened (credit balance)		21,980
Trial balance totals agree until error(s) found	121,780	121,780

Example 2 the trial balance does not balance. The larger amount is debit £121,780 and the smaller amount is credit £99,800. A credit amount of £121,780 - £99,800 = £21,980 is missing. A suspense account is opened as £21,980 credit balance to ensure the trial balance agrees and until the error(s) has been found.

Task 1 (21 marks)

Part (a) (18 marks)

Description /Serial number	Acquisition date	Cost £	Depreciation charges £	Carrying amount £	Funding method	Disposal proceeds £	Disposal date
Plant and machinery							
Machine AX56	01/09/X4	13000.00			Loan		
Year ended 31/08/X5			3250.00	9750.00			
Year ended 31/08/X6			2437.50	7312.50			
Year ended 31/08/X7			0.00	0.00		2000.00	24/07/X7
Machine AZ50	**01/09/X6**	**21390.00**			**Part Exchange**		
Year ended 31/08/X7			**5347.50**	**16042.50**			
Motor vehicles							
Car EN65 RBV	23/01/X6	6700.00			Loan		
Year ended 31/08/X6			2345.00	4355.00			
Year ended 31/08/X7			**1524.25**	**2830.75**			
Car BN60 DFV	26/08/X5	7800.00			Finance lease		
Year ended 31/08/X5			2730.00	5070.00			
Year ended 31/08/X6			1774.50	3295.50			
Year ended 31/08/X7			**1153.43**	**2142.07**			

Tutor notes and workings:

To: A.N. Business	From: Z Business Invoice number: 1123	Date: 1 Sept 20X6
Item	**Details**	**£**
Machine AZ50	AZ50	**19,000.00**
Software	for AZ50	**1,290.00**
2 x PC Monitors (screens)	@ £150 each for AZ50	**300.00**
Delivery and installation	for AZ50	**800.00**
Net total		**21,390.00**
VAT 20%		4,278.00
Total		25,668.00

Machine AX56 (sold)

- This machine would be removed from the accounting records of the business by posting both the cost and accumulated depreciation for this asset to a disposal account. The carrying value would be zero since the asset has been removed.
- Depreciation charged is 0.00 because the accounting policy of the business is to apply none in the year of disposal.
- Disposal proceeds would be recorded in the non-current asset register excluding any VAT. The VAT on the transaction would have been posted to the VAT control account for the period.
- The correct date of sale (disposal) is required to be entered in the non-current asset register.

Machine AZ50 (purchased)

Capitalisation of cost for this machine

- Machine AZ50 £19,000 is capital expenditure.
- The software and 2 monitors are also capital expenditure. Even the though the monitors are below the cost £200 each (the accounting policy of capitalising expenditure), machine AZ50 'in aggregate' (in total) costs more than £200 for all items relating to this machine. The entire purchase cost should be capitalised.
- Delivery and installation cost is always treated as capital expenditure along with the asset.
- VAT should be ignored as the business will reclaim all VAT from the purchase price of the asset. The VAT on the transaction would have been posted to the VAT control account for the period.
- Total cost ignoring VAT that should be capitalised (items highlighted in red bold in the invoice above) should be £21,390.00.

Depreciation charges for machine AZ50

- Plant and machinery is depreciated at 25% per annum on a diminishing balance basis.
- A full year's depreciation is applied in the year of acquisition.
- £21,390 is the carrying value (and original cost as it has just been acquired) x 25% = £5,347.50 depreciation charged.
- The carrying value at the year-end is Cost £21,390.00 - Accumulated depreciation £5,347.50 = £16,042.50.

Car EN65 RBV

- Motor vehicles are depreciated at 35% per annum on a diminishing balance basis.
- The carrying value of the car at the beginning of the year was £4,355.00 x 35% depreciation rate = £1,524.25 depreciation charges.
- The carrying value at the beginning of the year was £4,355.00 less depreciation charged for the year £1524.25 = carrying value of the car at the end of the year £2830.75.

Car BN60 DFV

- Motor vehicles are depreciated at 35% per annum on a diminishing balance basis.
- The carrying value of this car at the beginning of the year was £3,295.50 x 35% depreciation rate = £1,153.43 depreciation charges.
- The carrying value of the car at the beginning of the year £3,295.50 less depreciation charges for the year £1,153.43 = carrying value of the car at the end of the year £2,142.07.

Part (b) (3 marks)

Carrying value at the beginning of the year	7312.50
Part exchange value	2000.00
Loss on disposal	-5312.50

There was a loss on disposal of machine AX56 due to the part exchange value being only £2,000, given as a reduction against the cost of the new asset. Proceeds were lower when compared to the carrying value of £7312.50. Whenever sale proceeds (cash or part exchange value) are less than the carrying value of the asset being sold, a loss will arise.

Task 2 (17 marks)

Part (a) (12 marks)

The straight-line method uses a constant amount of depreciation each year:

Straight Line Depreciation per annum = (Cost - Residual Value) / Useful Life of Asset.

Straight Line Depreciation per annum = (£18,930 - £2,000) / 5 years = £3,386 every year the same depreciation charge.

Machinery at cost

	£		£
Balance b/d	84900	Balance c/d	103830
Bank	18930		
	103830		103830

Machinery accumulated depreciation

	£		£
Balance c/d	52586	Balance b/d	49200
		Deprciation charges	3386
	52586		52586

Depreciation charges

	£		£
Balance b/d	22600	Profit or loss account	25986
Machinery accumulated depreciation	3386		
	25986		25986

Part (b) (2 marks)

Debit
Bank

Credit
Disposals

Part (c) (3 marks)

Gains or losses on disposal of non-current assets are calculated by comparing the carrying value of the asset (original cost - accumulated depreciation), to the proceeds received from sale (or disposal) of the asset.

The business made a **Loss** on the disposal of the van of £ | 3800 |

The carrying value of the van (original cost £18,000 - accumulated depreciation to date £12,600) was £5,400. It was sold for £1,600. So given it was sold for less than the carrying value there is a loss on disposal of the asset. The loss would be £5,400 carrying value less £1,600 sale proceeds = £3,800 loss on disposal.

Task 3 (19 marks)

(a) Complete the following statement.

(4 marks)

| Prepaid expenses ⬇ | of | £ | 300 | dated | 31/12/X7 ⬇ |

The £900 insurance payment is an expense consumed which relates to this accounting period and the next accounting period. The £900 paid relates to the period of time 1/5/X7 to 30/4/X8 (12 months). For the year ended 31 December 20X7, 1/1/X8 to 30/4/X8 (4 months) does not belong to this accounting period. The 4 months represents prepaid expenses in advance for the year ended. We would prorate in months how the amount for prepaid expenses for the year ended. £900 ÷ 12 months = £75 per month x 4 months = £300 prepaid expenses. This is an asset because the business has paid for expenses which it has not yet consumed any benefit from, but it will do so in the next accounting period.

All accruals or prepayments are provided as period end adjustments at the year ended, so entries to ledgers will always have the year-end date which is 31 December 20X7.

(b) Update the motor vehicle expenses account

(6 marks)

Motor vehicle expenses

	£		£
Bank	8042	Prepaid expenses	300
		Profit or loss account	7742
	8042		8042

Prepaid expenses are an asset in the statement of financial position. The double entry at the year ended is DR Prepaid expenses (asset) and CR motor vehicle expenses. This has the effect of reducing expenses by £300 which relates to the next accounting period.

(c) Enter the figures given in the table below in the appropriate trial balance columns.

(2 marks)

DEAD CLIC

Debit	Credit
Expenses	Liabilities
Assets	Income
Drawings	Capital

Extract from the trial balance

Account	Ledger balance	Trial balance	
	£	£ DR	£CR
Prepaid income (liability)	1000		1000
Drawings (see DEADCLIC) drawings a DR	8900	8900	
Carriage inwards (expense)	1029	1029	
Accrued income (asset)	1504	1504	

(d) Calculate bank interest received that will be shown as income in the statement of profit or loss for the year ended 31 December 20X7.

(4 marks)

The £26 interest earned relates to the period 01/12/X7 to 31/12/X7, but was not received until after the year ended 31 December 20X7. It is accrued income which is income earned but not received and therefore not recorded currently in the books of the business. There is no need to prorate in months because the £26 is for one month only.

We need to at the end of the year DR Accrued income £26 (asset in the financial position) and CR Interest received £26 (increasing income in the profit or loss account). Accrued income at the beginning of the year would be simply the reverse of this entry because you are reversing at the beginning of the year whatever you did on the last day of the previous year.

To understand the calculations needed to complete this task, the best approach would be to draw up a ledger account as a working to check the logic is correct.

Interest received

	£		£
Accrued income (reversal)	45	Bank	142
Profit or loss account	123	Accrued income	26
	168		168

	£
Cash book figure	142
Opening adjustment	-45
Closing adjustment	26
Bank interest received for the year ended 31/12/X7	123

£26 of accrued income for the year end (earned, but not received) is added to the £142 interest received in the period. The £45 accrued income (reversal) at the beginning of the year is deducted to find the income to be recognised in the profit or loss account for the period.

(e) Complete the following true or false statements

(3 marks)

	TRUE	FALSE
Accrued income provided at the year end will have the effect of increasing profits within the statement of profit or loss for the year.	☑	☐
Prepaid income is a current asset included within the statement of financial position.	☐	☑
Accrued expenses are a current liability included within the statement of financial position.	☑	☐

- The first statement is true (refer to accrued income in the above task), it is a credit to income and therefore income will increase and therefore profits will increase.
- The second statement is false as prepaid income is a liability (DR Income CR Prepaid income), it is money received (recorded) which has not been earned until the next accounting period.
- The third statement is true, the double entry is to increase DR expenses and increase CR liabilities (accrued expenses), for expenses consumed but not yet paid for and not recorded in the books of the business.

Task 4 (23 marks)

(a) Refer to the extract from the extended trial balance below. Calculate the value of the adjustment required (to the nearest £).

(2 marks)

£ | 82 |

The allowance for doubtful debts account is an opposite account to the SLCA and both are represented together in the financial position (SLCA is a debit balance and the allowance for doubtful debts a credit balance). Both accounts will be offset to find the net amount owed by credit customers. Similar to how we offset accumulated depreciation against the original cost of a non-current asset to find the carrying value of the asset.

The allowance for doubtful debts is calculated by applying a percentage expected for doubtful debts against the SLCA (asset) balance after accounting for any irrecoverable debts. In this question irrecoverable debts have already been provided for so the SLCA is £24,090 after irrecoverable debts have been adjusted for.

The allowance for doubtful debts for the year end must be 2% of the SLCA (£24,090 x 2% = £482). The current balance for the allowance for doubtful debts is a credit of £400. This credit balance needs to be increased to £482 credit (currently £400 credit), so we need to credit £82 to the increase the allowance for doubtful debts. The other side of the double entry always goes to the allowance for doubtful debts - adjustment which is represented in the profit or loss account.

- DR £82 allowance for doubtful debts - adjustment (profit or loss).
- CR £82 allowance for doubtful debts (financial position).

(b) Record the adjustment in (a) and the following adjustments in the extract from the extended trial balance below.

(14 marks)

- Office expenses of £90 have been correctly posted to the cashbook but no corresponding debit entry was made to office expenses. **Debit office expenses £90 and credit suspense account £90.** This is a single sided error where a credit to the cash book was made but no debit entry, so the suspense account holds a £90 debit entry until this is reversed.
- The purchase ledger control account in the general ledger has been extracted and included in the trial balance incorrectly as £5,999. The correct balance to be included is £6,739. £6,739 - £5,999 = PLCA £740 understated as a credit balance. **We need to credit another £740 to the PLCA. We need to debit the suspense account £740.** If £5,999 only was included as a credit in the trial balance, then £740 credit would be included in the suspense account to ensure the trial balance will balance. We now have reversed this entry.
- Staff wages of £1,080 were in error posted to office expenses. **Take £1,080 out of office expenses (credit to reduce the expense) and include in staff wages (debit to increase the expense) £1,080.** No imbalance between debits and credits exist with this error so no suspense account entry is required.

Ledger account	Ledger balances		Adjustments	
	Dr £	Cr £	Dr £	Cr £
Bank	21932			
Opening inventory	6781			
Irrecoverable debts	750			
Capital		24976		
Office expenses	4200		90	1080
Staff wages	16339		1080	
Allowance for doubtful debts		400		82
Allowance for doubtful debts - adjustment			82	
Depreciation charges	2952			
Van at cost	17400			
Van accumulated depreciation		6090		
Purchases	45688			
Purchase ledger control account		5999		740
Sales		79991		
Sales ledger control account	24090			
Suspense		650	740	90

(c) Show the journal entries that will be required to close off the purchase ledger control account for the year ended 31 December 20X7 and select an appropriate narrative.

(4 marks)

The purchase ledger control account in the general ledger is now £6,739 credit. It is a liability in the statement of financial position and must be balanced and transferred to it.

Journal

Account	Dr £	Cr £
Purchases ledger control account	6739	
Statement of financial position		6739

Narrative for journal

Transfer to the statement of financial position

(d) Show the journal entries that will be required to adjust for closing inventory of £13,422 for the year ended 31 December 20X7.

(3 marks)

Account	Dr £	Cr £
Closing inventory (statement of financial position)	13422	
Closing inventory (statement of profit or loss account)		13422

Closing inventory is a credit to the statement of profit or loss account. It reduces purchases and therefore cost of sales, for the cost of unsold goods at the year end. This adjustment ensures that only the purchase cost of inventory which has been sold will be matched against sales earned for the same period. Closing inventory (goods held for resale) is also an asset (debit) in the statement of financial position.

Task 5 (20 marks)

Part (a) 6 marks

This task can examine adjustments to a sales ledger control account (SLCA), purchase ledger control account (PLCA) or the cash book from reconciliations already undertaken in the task.

Account	Dr £	Cr £
Adjustment 1		1000
Adjustment 2	11280	
Adjustment 3		240

1.	The total column of the purchase daybook was undercast by £1,000. The amount posted to the purchase ledger control account was £131,673 and the correct amount should be £132,673. **The total column of the purchases daybook would be credited to the PLCA. Given the total was undercast (under added) by £1,000 then we need to post £1,000 more to the PLCA. CR PLCA £1,000 to increase liabilities to suppliers.**
2.	Purchase returns of £5,640 have been credited to the purchase ledger control account in error. The correct entries have been made in the purchases ledger accounts of suppliers. **Purchase returns should be a debit, not credit to the PLCA because they reduce liability to pay suppliers. We need to debit £5,640 to cancel the error and then debit again £5,640 to record the amount correctly (2 x £5,640) = £11,280 DR PLCA.**
3.	A purchase invoice of £240 from Streets Ltd was omitted from purchases daybook. The correct entry was made in the purchase ledger account of the supplier. **The purchases daybook would be used to credit the PLCA with the total of supplier invoices. Given £240 was omitted then we need to post another £240 more to the PLCA. CR PLCA £240 to increase liability to suppliers.**
4.	A set-off entry of £5,042 was omitted from the purchase ledger account of M. Smith. The correct entry was made in purchases ledger control account. **The PLCA has been correctly updated but the purchase ledger account of the supplier needs to be reduced by £5,042.**
5.	Purchase returns of £120 was debited in error to the purchase ledger account of Winkle Traders Ltd instead of the purchase ledger account of Traders RUS Ltd. **The wrong supplier account but a correct posting was made to the PLCA. Both the PLCA and purchase ledger balances would still agree.**
6.	A purchase invoice was sent by a supplier for £360 in error, the correct amount should have been £3,600. The incorrect amount of £360 was posted to both the purchases ledger and purchases ledger control account. **This is a supplier error and both the PLCA and purchases ledger has been updated by £360. When the correct invoice is received then both ledgers will be adjusted but currently both balances will still agree as they contain an entry for the same amount.**

A PLCA showing the adjustments and the reconciliation (agreement) to the total balances in the purchase ledger accounts has been shown below to aid logic and further understanding.

PLCA (Trade Payables)

	£		£
Adjustment 2	11280	Balance b/d	27042
Balance c/d	17002	Adjustment 1	1000
		Adjustment 3	240
	28282		28282

Adjustments to purchase ledger accounts

	£
Total balances from purchase ledger accounts	22044
Adjustment 4	-5042
Revised (corrected) balance from PLCA	17002

Adjustments 5 and 6 are not reconciling items and therefore ignored in the process above.

Part (b) 3 marks

Integrity	☐
Professional competence and due care	☑
Confidentiality	☐

AAT members and students should work to the best of their ability, diligently and with due care when performing tasks or giving advice. Without competence, then work must be done by supervision or review by someone who is an expert. To advise about this matter without competence would be in breach of professional competence and due care. There is nothing here to suggest a breach of confidentiality or being dishonest (lack of integrity) if VAT advice was given.

Part (c) 11 marks

Tutor note: the trial balance has two adjustments for closing inventory. The DR (an asset) for closing inventory to be included in the statement of financial position and a CR (reduction to purchases expenses) for closing inventory to be included within the statement of profit or loss for the year ended.

The exam will have autosum function for the trial balance totals, so you will not need to add up your columns in the exam task. There is also a picklist selection for the profit or loss for the year end which when the amount is included it should balance the last 4 columns of the ETB. If a profit for example below, then the profit amount is a debit to the statement of profit or loss (closing the profit or loss account for the year) and a credit (transfer) to the statement of financial position (increasing the capital account balance owed to the owner of the business).

Ledger account	Ledger balances		Adjustments		Statement of profit or loss		Statement of financial position	
	Dr £	Cr £	Dr £	Cr £	Dr £	Cr £	Dr £	Cr £
Purchases	13870			1200	12670			
Purchase ledger control account		4520	2300					2220
Sales		80242				80242		
Sales ledger control account	13298			2300			10998	
Staff wages	27581			6000	21581			
Bank	40211			56			40155	
Allowance for doubtful debts: adjustment			450		450			
Allowance for doubtful debts		1846		450				2296
Purchases returns		740				740		
Office expenses	5698		56		5754			
Closing inventory			1042	1042		1042	1042	
Depreciation charges			4000		4000			
Office equipment at cost	20000						20000	
Office equipment accumulated depreciation		12000		4000				16000
Opening inventory	930				930			
VAT		3241						3241
Capital		30999						30999
Drawings	12000		7200				19200	
Profit/loss for the year					36639			36639
Total	133588	133588	15048	15048	82024	82024	91395	91395

Mock Exam Two
AAT L3 Advanced Book-keeping

Assessment information:

You have **2 hours** to complete this practice assessment.

This assessment contains **5 tasks** and you should attempt to complete **every** task.
Each task is independent. You will not need to refer to your answers to previous tasks.
Read every task carefully to make sure you understand what is required.

The standard rate of VAT is 20%.

Where the date is relevant, it is given in the task data.
Both minus signs and brackets can be used to indicate negative numbers **unless** task instructions say otherwise.

You must use a full stop to indicate a decimal point. For example, write 100.57 not 100,57 or 100 57
You may use a comma to indicate a number in the thousands, but you don't have to.
For example, 10000 and 10,000 are both acceptable.

Task 1 (21 marks)

This task is about non-current assets.

You are working on the accounting records of a business known as BZ Trading.

BZ Trading is a VAT registered business.

BZ Trading purchased a new van during the accounting period. The following is the relevant purchase invoice.

To: BZ Trading	From: XPD Cars & Vans Invoice number: 099	Date: 3 December 20X7
Item	**Details**	**£**
Van Q3	Q3 model	12,950.00
Alloy wheels and roof rack	for Q3 model	1,290.00
Business signage on van	for Q3 model	299.00
Delivery		129.00
12 months road fund licence		225.00
Net total		14,893.00
VAT 20%		2978.60
Total		17,871.60
Finance lease arrangement 27.6% interest rate per annum.		

VAT can be reclaimed on the purchase of the new van.

The following relates to a van which was sold by the business during the year.

Item description	Van MN64 XCT
Date of purchase	01/02/X6
Date of sale	24/07/X7
Cash received	£1,000.00 + VAT

BZ Trading has a policy of capitalising expenditure over £500.

- Plant and machinery is depreciated at 40% per annum on a diminishing balance basis.
- Motor vehicles are depreciated at 25% per annum on a diminishing balance basis.
- Fixtures and fittings are depreciated over ten years on a straight-line basis assuming no residual value.

Depreciation is calculated on an annual basis and charged in equal instalments for each full month an asset is owned for during the year.

(a) For the year ended 31 March 20X8, record the following in an extract of the non-current asset register shown below.

- Any acquisitions of non-current assets
- Any disposals of non-current assets
- Depreciation charges

Note: Not every cell will require an entry and not all cells will accept entries. Choose answers where a grey picklist is given and insert figures into highlighted grey cells.
Show your numerical answers to TWO decimal places.
Use DD/MM/YY format for any dates.

(18 marks)

Description /Serial number	Acquisition date	Cost £	Depreciation charges £	Carrying amount £	Funding method	Disposal proceeds £	Disposal date
Motor vehicles							
Van MN64 XCT	01/02/X6	8000.00			Cash		
Year ended 31/03/X6			333.33	7666.67			
Year ended 31/03/X7			1916.67	5750.00			
Year ended 31/03/X8							
Picklist 3 ⬇					Picklist 4 ⬇		
Year ended 31/03/X8							
Plant and machinery							
Refrigerator EN65	27/02/X7	12000.00			Loan		
Year ended 31/03/X7			4800.00	7200.00			
Year ended 31/03/X8							
Fixtures and fittings							
Shop furniture	06/05/X4	17800.00			Loan		
Year ended 31/03/X5			1483.33	16316.67			
Year ended 31/03/X6			1780.00	14536.67			
Year ended 31/03/X7			1780.00	12756.67			
Year ended 31/03/X8			Picklist 1 ⬇	Picklist 2 ⬇			

Picklist 1 ⬇	Picklist 2 ⬇	Picklist 3 ⬇	Picklist 4 ⬇
0.00	17800.00	Shop furniture	Cash
1780.00	10976.67	Refrigerator EN65	Finance Lease
1483.33	0.00	Van Q3	Hire Purchase
1523.00	12756.67	Van MN64 XCT	Loan

(b) Complete the following calculation (3 marks)

Fixtures and fittings above use the straight-line method of depreciation, calculate the straight-line depreciation rate charged per annum, as a percentage.

% ☐

End of Task

Task 2 (17 marks)

This task is about ledger accounting for non-current assets.

You are working on the accounting records of a business for the year ended 31 March 20X6. VAT can be ignored.

- An old motor vehicle was sold on 3 September 20X5 for £4,000, to help fund the purchase of a new motor vehicle. The sale proceeds were paid into the business bank account on the same day.
- The old motor vehicle was purchased for £13,800 on 13 March 20X4.
- A new motor vehicle was purchased for £18,250 and was paid for from the business bank account on 23 March 20X6.
- Motor vehicles are depreciated at ‚25% per annum on a diminishing balance basis.
- A full year's depreciation is charged in the year of acquisition and none in the year of disposal.

(a) Complete the following tasks relating to the old motor vehicle.   (9 marks)

(i) Calculate the accumulated depreciation to the nearest £ [   ]

(ii) Complete the disposals account shown below. Show clearly the balance to be carried down or transferred to the statement of profit or loss, as appropriate.

Picklist: Bank, Depreciation charges, Disposals, Vehicles accumulated depreciation, Vehicles at cost, Suspense, Profit or loss account, Purchases ledger control account, Purchases, Vehicle running expenses, Balance b/d, Balance c/d.

Disposals

	£		£
⇕		⇕	
⇕		⇕	
⇕		⇕	
	0		0

(b) Drag and drop the account names shown below to the debit and credit columns, to show the accounting entries for the purchase of the new motor vehicle.

(2 marks)

Disposals

Motor vehicles at cost

Bank

Debit

Credit

(c) Calculate depreciation charges for the new motor vehicle for the year ended 31 March 20X6 and show the journal entries required. Depreciation should be calculated to the nearest £.

(3 marks)

Account	Amount £	Debit	Credit
⬇			
⬇			

Picklist: Bank, Depreciation charges, Disposals, Vehicles accumulated depreciation, Vehicles at cost, Suspense, Profit or loss account, Purchases ledger control account, Purchases, Vehicle running expenses, Balance b/d, Balance c/d.

(d) If the old motor vehicle was used as part-exchange against the cost of the new motor vehicle. Drag and drop the account names to the debit and credit columns to show where the entries for the part-exchange amount would be made.

(3 marks)

Disposals

Motor vehicles at cost

Bank

Debit

Credit

End of Task

Task 3 (19 marks)

This task is about ledger accounting, including accruals and prepayments.

(a) Enter the figures given in the table below in the appropriate trial balance columns.

Do not enter zeros in unused column cells. Do not enter any figures as negative.

(2 marks)

Extract from the trial balance

Account	Ledger balance £	Trial balance £ DR	£CR
Accrued income	670		
Carriage outwards	312		
Discounts received	1229		
Prepaid income	1500		

You are working on the accounting records of a business for the year ended 30 September 20X7.

In this task, you can ignore VAT.

> **Business policy: accounting for accruals and prepayments**
> An entry is made to the income or expense account and an opposite entry to the relevant asset or liability account. In the following period, asset or liability entries are reversed.

You are looking at rental income earned by the business for the year.

- The cash book for the year shows receipts for rental income of £36,000.
- This includes £4,500 for the period 01/09/X7 to 30/11/X7.

(b) Update the rental income account shown below.

Show clearly:

- **the cash book figure**
- **the year end adjustment**
- **the transfer to the statement of profit or loss for the year.**

(6 marks)

Rental income

	£		£
⮃		Prepaid income (reversal)	7500
⮃		⮃	
⮃		⮃	
	0		7500

> **Picklist:** Rent expenses, Rental income, Bank, Accrued expenses, Accrued income, Accrued income (reversal), Accrued expenses (reversal), Prepaid income, Statement of financial position, Prepaid income (reversal), Prepaid expenses (reversal), Profit or loss account, Prepaid expenses, Purchases ledger control account, Sales, Sales ledger control account, Balance b/d, Balance c/d.

(c) Answer the following regarding the prepaid income reversal of £7,500 in (b) above.

(4 marks)

(i) How are the elements of the accounting equation effected by this transaction. Tick ONE box for each row.

	Increase	Decrease	No change
Assets	☐	☐	☐
Liabilities	☐	☐	☐
Capital	☐	☐	☐

(ii) Which ONE of the following dates should be entered for this transaction in the ledger accounts.

30 September 20X7   ☐

1 October 20X6   ☐

30 September 20X6   ☐

You are looking at motor vehicle expenses for the year.

- The cash book shows payments for motor vehicle expenses during the year of £13,102.
- Cash book payments do not include £957 for motor expenses. The invoice dated 29 September 20X7 was not received or paid until after the year ended.
- The business had accrued motor vehicle expenses of £798 at the beginning of the accounting period.

(d) (i) Calculate the motor vehicle expenses for the year ended 30 September 20X7 and complete the table shown below. If necessary, use a minus sign to indicate ONLY the deduction of an amount from the cash book figure.

(4 marks)

	£
Cash book figure	
Opening adjustment	
Closing adjustment	
Motor vehicle expenses for the year ended 30/09/X7	

(d) (ii) Drag and drop the account names to the debit and credit columns to show the accounting entries for accrued motor expenses (reversal) at the beginning of the accounting period.

(3 marks)

Accrued expenses
Profit or loss account
Motor vehicle expenses

Debit	Credit

- -

End of Task

Task 4 (23 marks)

This task is about accounting adjustments. You are working as an accounting technician on the accounting records of a business with a year ended of 31 May 20X3. A trial balance has been drawn up and a suspense account opened.

You now need to make some corrections and adjustments for the year ended.

You may ignore VAT in this task.

Record the journal entries required within the general ledger to deal with the items below.

You should:

- **remove any incorrect entries as appropriate.**
- **post the correct entries.**

Note: You do NOT need to give narratives.
Do NOT enter zeros into unused column cells.

> **Picklist for all journals below:** Rent expenses, Rental income, Bank, Accrued expenses, Statement of financial position, Prepaid expenses, Irrecoverable debts, Buildings at cost, Premises expenses, Profit or loss account, Purchases ledger control account, Sales, Sales ledger control account, Suspense, Allowance for doubtful debts, Allowance for doubtful debts - adjustment, Balance b/d, Balance c/d.

(a) Entries for prepaid rent expenses of £1,500 were made. The entries were on the correct side of both relevant general ledger accounts, but a figure of only £1,050 was incorrectly posted to prepaid expenses.

(6 marks)

Account	Dr £	Cr £

(b) No entries have been made to the allowance for doubtful debts account. Allowance for doubtful debts needs to be 5% of trade receivables. Trade receivables for the year ended was £24,000.

(6 marks)

Account	Dr £	Cr £
⬇		
⬇		

(c) A returned cheque by the bank of £840 from a credit customer was correctly entered into the bank account. No other entries were made.

(3 marks)

Account	Dr £	Cr £
⬇		
⬇		

(d) Premises repairs costing £720 were paid for by BACS. The correct amount was credited to the bank account and incorrectly debited to the buildings at cost account.

(3 marks)

Account	Dr £	Cr £
⬇		
⬇		

(e) Which TWO of the following statements about suspense accounts are TRUE.

(2 marks)

used where a proper account cannot be determined at the time a transaction was recorded	☐
an account in the general ledger in which amounts are temporarily recorded	☐
indicates that the trial balance is free from errors and omissions	☐
should continue to appear in the general ledger for the business	☐

Barry is an accounting technician working in accountancy practice, he performs book-keeping services for both clients ABC Ltd and XYX Ltd. These two companies are in dispute about a series of purchases that XYZ Ltd has made from ABC Ltd.

(f) Identify which of the fundamental ethical principles is threatened if Barry continues to act for both companies. Choose ONE answer only.

(3 marks)

a) objectivity and confidentiality
b) integrity and professional behaviour
c) confidentiality and professional competence

End of Task

Task 5 (20 marks)

This task is about period end routines, using accounting records, ethical principles and the extended trial balance.

Jim is an AAT student working for a firm of accountants, one particular client that Jim is completing some tax work for has asked Jim to overlook some tax issues and to record for tax purposes less money than the client has actually banked in the year. The client has promised Jim a really nice gift tomorrow if Jim agrees to do this.

(a) What should Jim do to avoid being in breach of the fundamental ethical principles. Choose ONE answer.

    a) Accept the offer of the gift and then keep quiet about the tax issues.
    b) Confirm all issues the client wants Jim to overlook before Jim accepts the gift.
    c) Reject the offer of the gift and continue to review the clients records thoroughly.

You are preparing a sales ledger control account reconciliation for a sole trader as at 31 August 20X8.

The balance showing on sales ledger control account is a debit of £13,042. Total customer account balances in the sales ledger is a debit of £11,540.

The sales ledger has been compared with sales ledger control account and the following adjustments have been identified:

1.	The total column of the sales daybook was overcast by £1,100. The amount posted to the sales ledger control account was £81,670, the correct amount that should have been posted is £80,570.
2.	Sales returns of £1,220 have been credited to the sales ledger account of WX Traders Ltd instead of the sales ledger account of Mr Wren.
3.	A sales invoice of £34 for Strands Trading Ltd was omitted from the sales daybook. The correct entry was made in the sales ledger account of the customer.
4.	A set-off entry of £504 was omitted from the sales ledger account of E. Barry. The correct entry was made in the sales ledger control account.
5.	Sales returns of £640 were in error debited to the sales ledger control account. The correct entry was made in the sales ledger account of the customer.
6.	An irrecoverable debt of £340 has been written off in the sales ledger control account. No entry was made in the sales ledger account of the customer.

(b) Use the following table to show the THREE adjustments that should appear in the sales ledger control account. Enter only ONE figure for each line. Do not enter zeros in unused cells.

(6 marks)

Account	Dr £	Cr £
⬇		
⬇		
⬇		

Picklist: Adjustment 1, Adjustment 2, Adjustment 3, Adjustment 4, Adjustment 5, Adjustment 6.

You are now working on the accounting records of a different business.

You have the following extended trial balance. The adjustments have already been correctly entered.

(c) Extend the figures into the columns for the statement of profit or loss and the statement of financial position. Do NOT enter zeros into unused column cells. Complete the extended trial balance by totalling the columns and entering any profit or loss figure for the year ended.

(11 marks)

Extended trial balance

Ledger account	Ledger balances		Adjustments		Statement of profit or loss		Statement of financial position	
	Dr £	Cr £	Dr £	Cr £	Dr £	Cr £	Dr £	Cr £
Bank		4103						4103
Opening inventory	8900				8900			
Prepayments			400				400	
Capital		11500						11500
Motor vehicle expenses	6722			1400	5322			
Staff wages	28039				28039			
Irrecoverable debts			6000		6000			
Depreciation charges			21508		21508			
Sales returns	1720			900	820			
Telephone expenses	1321			400	921			
Closing inventory			4300	4300		4300	4300	
VAT		3251						3251
Motor vehicle at cost	60050		1400				61450	
Motor vehicle accumulated depreciation		21017		21508				42525
Purchases	55430		1680		57110			
Purchase ledger control account		24591						24591
Sales		124000				124000		
Sales ledger control account	25500			6000			19500	
Suspense	780		900	1680				
Profit/loss for the year						320	320	
Total	188462	188462	36188	36188	128620	128620	85970	85970

Picklist
Profit/loss for the year
Suspense
Balance b/d
Balance c/d
Gross profit/loss for the year

End of Task

Mock Exam Two - Solutions

AAT L3 Advanced Book-keeping

You may find the following tutor notes useful when answering exam practice tasks.

Elements of the financial statements

Five elements make up the general ledger accounts and financial statements of a business.

Assets

A resource controlled by the business as a result of past events and from which future economic benefits (money) are expected to flow to the business.

- Premises, machines, motor vehicles, office equipment or furniture and fittings.
- Inventory currently for resale.
- Trade receivables (money to be 'received') also called sales ledger control account.
- Accrued income.
- Prepaid expenses.
- Money in the bank.
- Cash in hand.

Liabilities

A present obligation of the business arising from past events, the settlement of which is expected to result in an outflow from the business.

- VAT owed to HMRC
- Wages owed to staff
- Bank loans and overdrafts
- Trade payables (money to be 'paid') also called purchases ledger control account.
- Prepaid income.
- Accrued expenses.

Capital

The residual interest (whatever is left) from the assets of the business after deducting all of its liabilities. Total assets less total liabilities is equal to capital (also called 'net assets') of the business. This balance represents what is owed and accumulated by the business to its owner. A separate account for drawings can also be maintained in the general ledger, drawings is money taken from the business by the owner and rather than reducing the owners capital account for the money taken, a drawings account is kept as a separate account because it provides more information.

Income

Money earned or received by the business from the sale of goods or services that is makes or sells (its trade), or from other investments or trade sources.

- Cash sales (sales not on credit).
- Credit sales (sales on credit).
- Rent received from ownership and rental of premises.
- Bank interest received.
- Discounts received (PPD) from paying credit suppliers early.
- Commission received.

Expenses

Costs incurred or paid for by the business in the normal course of trade in order to earn income. The cost of goods sold and other expenses must be matched with the sales revenues earned in the same period.

- Cash purchases (inventory purchases for resale and not on credit).
- Credit purchases (inventory purchases for resale and on credit).
- Rent payments (if the business is renting a property).
- Staff wages
- Motor vehicle running costs.
- Advertising.
- Depreciation such as wear and tear or loss of value to long-term assets such as machines or motor vehicles.
- Bank interest and charges.
- Discounts allowed (PPD) to credit customers who pay early.
- Accountancy and legal services.
- Irrecoverable debts expense.
- Increase (debit)/Decrease (credit) in allowances for doubtful debts.

Income and expenses are used to work out the amount of profit the business has generated. Any profits are owed to the owner of the business and increase the capital account of the owner.

DEAD CLIC

Don't get clouded in the double entry logic, ledgers are balances kept for the five elements of the financial statements and we are increasing or decreasing these balances according to the rules of double entry.

Important double entry terminology

DEAD CLIC defines what is the 'normal balance' or the natural state for a T account (general, sales or purchase ledger account).

DEAD CLIC is an acronym which gives the elements of financial statements and whether each element would be a debit or credit balance overall within a double entry ledger system. It can be used for determining the correct debit or credit balance but the element must be determined first. It can also be used to determine the correct double entry to increase or decrease an account balance.

DEAD CLIC

Debit	Credit
Expenses	Liabilities
Assets	Income
Drawings	Capital

The elements	Natural state	Increase balance (as per the natural state)	Decrease balance (opposite to natural state)
Income	Credit	Credit	Debit
Expenses	Debit	Debit	Credit
Assets	Debit	Debit	Credit
Liabilities	Credit	Credit	Debit
Capital	Credit	Credit	Debit

Totalling and balancing ledger accounts

1. Look at both sides of the ledger account and find the side which has the biggest total amount (debits or credits).
2. Add up the 'total' of all the entries on the side that has the biggest total amount and put this 'total' amount on both sides of the ledger account.
3. Add up all the entries on the side of the ledger account that had the smallest total amount.
4. Work out on the side that had the smallest total amount, the difference between the total amount entered and the other entries made on this side. This is the balance carried down (c/d) at the end of the period.
5. The balance c/d is entered on the side of the ledger account that had the smallest total amount to ensure that both total amounts entered on either side of the ledger account agrees. This as an arithmetical control and considered good practice in manual ledger accounting.

The balance c/d is only a balancing figure to ensure both sides of the ledger account agree at the end of the period. The true debit or credit balance is brought down (b/d) on the opposite side to the balance carried down (c/d). The balance b/d is on the 1st (beginning) of the month and the balance c/d is at the end of the month 30th/31st (ignoring February).

The trial balance and errors

The purpose of a trial balance is to ensure that all entries made in an organisation's general ledger are properly balanced and to check the accuracy of entries made before a final set of financial accounts are produced. If the totals for debit and credit balances do not agree then errors have definitely occurred, but even if the totals for debit and credit balances do agree it does not guarantee the general ledger balances are free from errors or omissions.

Types of errors not disclosed by the trial balance

The following types of error all have one thing in common, the same amount has been debited and credited within the general ledger, but an error has still occurred. These type of errors do not cause an imbalance when a trial balance is prepared (total debits equal total credits in the trial balance). Types of errors not disclosed by the trial balance can be remembered using the acronym 'TOPCROC'. Because the trial balance will still balance these types of error are more difficult to detect.

- **T Transposition** (two or more digits are reversed when amounts are entered).
- **O Original entry** (errors occur when documents such as invoices or credit notes are prepared incorrectly or when erroneous documents are posted to the day books).
- **P Principle** (mis posting to the WRONG ledger account and WRONG financial element), for example an 'expense' debited instead to an 'asset', a fundamental error because assets and profits will be under or overstated.
- **C Commission** (mis posting to the WRONG ledger account but RIGHT financial element), for example an 'expense' debited instead to another type of 'expense', less fundamental than an error of principle because assets and profits will be not be under or overstated.
- **R Reversal of entries** (the debit and credit mis posted the wrong way around).
- **O Omission** of a transaction (no posting made in the general ledger).
- **C Compensating** errors (very rare but this can happen), two independent errors for two different amounts posted as a debit and credit, the two errors compensate and cancel each other out. The trial balance will still balance.

Types of errors disclosed by the trial balance

The following types of error all have one thing in common, they all cause an imbalance when a trial balance is prepared (total debits do not equal total credits in the trial balance). Types of errors disclosed by the trial balance can be remembered using the acronym 'TESCOS'.

- **T Transposition** e.g. error posted incorrectly on one side of a ledger account but correctly posted on the other side such as debit expenses £54 and credit bank £45.
- **E Extraction** e.g. a ledger balance is not totalled and balanced correctly, so the wrong ledger balance is now 'extracted' and represented incorrectly in the trial balance.
- **S Single entry** e.g. a debit entry posted, but no credit entry posted, or vice versa.
- **C Casting** (casting means 'adding') e.g. a column in a day book casted (added up) incorrectly and the incorrect amount posted to the general ledger.
- **O Omission** of a ledger balance within the trial balance e.g. a ledger balance completely missed out and not included in the trial balance.
- **S Same sided** e.g. 2 debit entries only posted in error, or 2 credit entries only posted in error, rather than a debit and a credit entry made correctly.

Examples of how suspense accounts are opened

Example 1

Trial Balance (totals before suspense account opened)	154,896	155,279
Suspense account opened (debit balance)	383	
Trial balance totals agree until error(s) found	155,279	155,279

Example 1 the trial balance does not balance. The suspense account is always opened for the difference that exists between debits and credits and to ensure debits equal credits. The larger amount is credit £155,279 and the smaller amount is debit £154,896. A debit amount of £155,279 - £154,896 = £383 is missing. A suspense account is opened as £383 debit balance to ensure the trial balance agrees and until the error(s) has been found.

Example 2

Trial Balance (totals before suspense account opened)	121,780	99,800
Suspense account opened (credit balance)		21,980
Trial balance totals agree until error(s) found	121,780	121,780

Example 2 the trial balance does not balance. The larger amount is debit £121,780 and the smaller amount is credit £99,800. A credit amount of £121,780 - £99,800 = £21,980 is missing. A suspense account is opened as £21,980 credit balance to ensure the trial balance agrees and until the error(s) has been found.

Task 1 (21 marks)

Part (a) (18 marks)

Description /Serial number	Acquisition date	Cost £	Depreciation charges £	Carrying amount £	Funding method	Disposal proceeds £	Disposal date
Motor vehicles							
Van MN64 XCT	01/02/X6	8000.00			Cash		
Year ended 31/03/X6			333.33	7666.67			
Year ended 31/03/X7			1916.67	5750.00			
Year ended 31/03/X8			359.38	0.00		1000.00	24/07/X7
Van Q3	03/12/X7	14668.00			Finance lease		
Year ended 31/03/X8			916.75	13751.25			
Plant and machinery							
Refrigerator EN65	27/02/X7	12000.00			Loan		
Year ended 31/03/X7			4800.00	7200.00			
Year ended 31/03/X8			2880.00	4320.00			
Fixtures and fittings							
Shop furniture	06/05/X4	17800.00			Loan		
Year ended 31/03/X5			1483.33	16316.67			
Year ended 31/03/X6			1780.00	14536.67			
Year ended 31/03/X7			1780.00	12756.67			
Year ended 31/03/X8			1780.00	10976.67			

Van MN64 XCT (sold)

- The van would be removed from the accounting records of the business by posting both the cost and accumulated depreciation to a disposal account. The carrying value would always be zero because the asset has been removed from the accounting records of the business.
- Depreciation is calculated on an annual basis and charged in equal instalments for each full month the asset is owned for in the year. Depreciation charged would be 25% per annum x carrying value at the beginning of the year £5,750.00 = £1,437.50 per annum. The van was owned in the accounting period 01/04/X7 to 24/07/X7 which was for '3 full months'. £1,437.50 per annum ÷ 12 months = £119.79166 per month x 3 months = £359.38 depreciation charges. Since you are dividing by 12 and multiplying by 3, a quicker calculation would be £1,437.50 x 3/12 = £359.38.

- Disposal proceeds would be recorded in the non-current asset register excluding any VAT. The VAT on this transaction would have been posted to the VAT control account.
- The correct date of sale (disposal) is also required to be entered in the non-current asset register.

Van Q3 (purchased)

To: BZ Trading	From: XPD Cars & Vans Invoice number: 099	Date: 3 December 20X7
Item	**Details**	**£**
Van Q3	Q3 model	**12,950.00**
Alloy wheels and roof rack	for Q3 model	**1,290.00**
Business signage on van	for Q3 model	**299.00**
Delivery		**129.00**
12 months road fund licence		225.00
Net total		14,893.00
VAT 20%		2978.60
Total		17,871.60
Finance lease arrangement 27.6% interest rate per annum.		

Cost 'capitalised' for the van

- Van Q3 £12,950 is capital expenditure.
- The alloy wheels, roof rack and business signage for the van are capital expenditure. Even the though the business signage for the van is below £500 (the accounting policy for capitalising expenditure), 'in aggregate' (in total) costs for the van and all items relating to it is more than £500, so the entire cost of all items belonging to and the van should be capitalised.
- Delivery cost is always treated as capital expenditure along with the asset.
- 12 months road fund licence is revenue not capital expenditure, as this cost would be consumed by the business within one year.
- VAT should be ignored as the business will reclaim all VAT on the purchase.
- Total cost ignoring VAT that should be capitalised (items highlighted in red bold in the invoice above) is £12,950.00 + £1,290.00 + £299.00 + £129.00 = £14,668.00.

Depreciation for the van

- Depreciation is calculated on an annual basis and charged in equal instalments for each full month the asset is owned for in the year. Depreciation charged annually would be 25% x carrying value at the date of purchase £14,668.00 = £3,667. The van was owned in the accounting period from 03/12/X7 to 31/03/X8 which was for '3 full months' in the accounting period. £3,667 x 3/12 = £916.75.
- The carrying value at the year-end would be £14,668.00 - £916.75 = £13,751.25.

Refrigerator EN65

- Plant and machinery is depreciated at 40% per annum on a diminishing balance basis.
- The carrying value at the beginning of the year £7,200.00 x 40% = £2,800.00 depreciation charges.
- The carrying value at the year-end would be carrying value at the beginning of the year £7,200.00 - £2,800.00 depreciation charged in the year = £4,320.00.

Shop furniture

- Fixtures and fittings are depreciated over ten years on a straight-line basis assuming no residual value. Depreciation charges would be (original cost less zero residual value) ÷ 10 years = £1,780.00 per year.
- Carrying value at the year-end would be carrying value at the beginning of the year £12,756.67 - £1,780.00 depreciation charged in the year = £10,976.67.

Part (b) (3 marks)

Fixtures and fittings above use the straight-line method of depreciation. £1,780 depreciation charge per annum ÷ £17,800 original cost x 100% = 10% depreciation rate per annum. Alternative workings can also use time rather than amounts, for example, 1 year ÷ 10 years useful life = 10% rate.

Task 2 (17 marks)

(a) Complete the following tasks relating to the old motor vehicle: (9 marks)

(i) Calculate the accumulated depreciation to the nearest £ | 6038 |

The old vehicle was purchased 13 March 20X4, so depreciation charges would have been applied for the year ended 31 March 20X4 and 31 March 20X5 (two year-ends). A full year's depreciation is applied in the year of acquisition which was the year ended 31 March 20X4 and the year ended 31 March 20X5 it was owned throughout the accounting period. No depreciation is charged in the year of disposal 31 March 20X6 according to the accounting policy.

- **31 March 20X4** £13,800 cost (carrying value) x 25% per annum on a diminishing balance basis = £3,450 depreciation charges.
- **31 March 20X5** carrying value (£13,800 - £3,450) = £10,350 x 25% per annum on a diminishing balance basis = £2,587.50 depreciation charges.
- Total **accumulated depreciation** for both accounting periods £3,450 + £2,587.50 = £6,038 (rounded to the nearest £).

(ii) Complete the disposals account. Show clearly the balance to be carried down or transferred to the statement of profit or loss, as appropriate.

Disposals

	£		£
Vehicles at cost	13800	Vehicles accumulated depreciation	6038
		Bank	4000
		Profit or loss account	3762
	13800		13800

(b) Drag and drop the account names shown below to the debit and credit columns, to show the accounting entries for the purchase of the new motor vehicle.

(2 marks)

Debit
Motor vehicles at cost

Credit
Bank

(c) Calculate depreciation charges for the new motor vehicle for the year ended 31 March 20X6 and show the journal entries required. Depreciation should be calculated to the nearest £.

(3 marks)

- The new motor vehicle was purchased for £18,250 and was paid from the bank on 23 March 20X6.
- Motor vehicles are depreciated at 25% per annum on a diminishing balance basis. A full year's depreciation is applied in the year of acquisition.
- Depreciation £18,250 x 25% per annum = £4,562.50. Rounded to £4,563.

Account	Amount £	Debit	Credit
Depreciation charges	4563	X	
Vehicles accumulated depreciation	4563		X

(d) If the old motor vehicle was used as part-exchange against the cost of the new motor vehicle. Drag and drop the account names to the debit and credit columns to show where the entries for the part-exchange amount would be made.

(3 marks)

Debit
Motor vehicles at cost

Credit
Disposals

Task 3 (19 marks)

(a) Enter the figures given in the table below in the appropriate trial balance columns.

Do not enter zeros in unused column cells. Do not enter any figures as negative.

(2 marks)

DEAD CLIC

Debit	Credit
Expenses	Liabilities
Assets	Income
Drawings	Capital

	Ledger balance	Trial balance	
Account	£	£ DR	£CR
Accrued income (asset)	670	670	
Carriage outwards (expense)	312	312	
Discounts received (income)	1229		1229
Prepaid income (liability)	1500		1500

(b) Update the rental income account.

Show clearly:

- **the cash book figure**
- **the year end adjustment**
- **the transfer to the statement of profit or loss for the year.** (6 marks)

Rental income of £4,500 relates to the period 01/09/X7 to 30/11/X7 (3 months). The year end of the business is 30 September 20X7. 01/09/X7 to 30/09/X7 is 1 month rent received and earned for the year ended 30 September 20X7. 01/10/X7 to 30/11/X7 is 2 months rental income received in the books of the business but not earned in the accounting period 30 September 20X7.

This is prepaid income and we need to pro rate the £4,500 to calculate how much has been received but not earned. £4,500 ÷ 3 months (01/09/X7 to 30/11/X7) = £1,500 per month x 2 months (01/10/X7 to 30/11/X7) = £3,000 prepaid income. This must be removed from income included in the profit or loss account for the year-ended and included as income earned in the next accounting period.

Prepaid income is money received but not earned in the accounting period. It is a liability since the business has not earned the money yet so £3,000 is still owed to the tenant for the year ended. The double entry to record this amount would be CR prepaid income (increase liabilities in the statement of financial position) and DR rental income (reduce income earned in the profit or loss account). In conclusion liabilities increase by £3,000 and income decreases by £3,000.

Rental income

	£		£
Prepaid income	3000	Prepaid income (reversal)	7500
Profit or loss account	40500	Bank	36000
	43500		43500

(c) Answer the following regarding the prepaid income reversal of £7,500 in (b) above.

(4 marks)

(i) How are the elements of the accounting equation effected by this transaction. Tick ONE box for each row.

A prepaid income (reversal) as an accounting entry at the beginning of the accounting period would be the opposite accounting entry made at the end of an accounting period. The double entry to record this amount would be DR £7,500 prepaid income (decrease liabilities in the statement of financial position) and CR £7,500 rental income (increase income earned in the profit or loss account). In conclusion liabilities now decrease and income now increases. If income increases, so will profits earned which will increase the capital account of the owner of the business.

	Increase	Decrease	No change
Assets	☐	☐	☑
Liabilities	☐	☑	☐
Capital	☑	☐	☐

(ii) Which ONE of the following dates should be entered for this transaction in the ledger accounts.

Accruals or prepayments are provided as period end adjustments at the year ended, so entries to ledgers will always have the year-end date which in this case is 30 September 20X7. Accruals or prepayments always reverse on the first day of the accounting period which in this case would be 1 October 20X6, so this date would be the ledger entry date for the £7,500 prepaid income reversal.

30 September 20X7	☐
1 October 20X6	☑
30 September 20X6	☐

(d) (i) Calculate the motor vehicle expenses for the year ended 30 September 20X7 and complete the table shown below. If necessary, use a minus sign to indicate ONLY the deduction of an amount from the cash book figure.

(4 marks)

To understand the logic of the calculations needed to complete this question, a good approach is to draw up a ledger account working. Bank payments of £13,102 are being adjusted for accrued expenses (expenses consumed but not paid for) to find the amount charged to the profit and loss account for the year ended. You can see from the account below that £957 is being added to £13,102 on the same side of the account and £798 is deducted (the opposite side of the account), to find the amount charged to the profit or loss account as an expense for the year-ended.

Workings

Motor vehicle expenses

	£		£
Bank	13102	Accrued expenses (reversal)	798
Accrued expenses	957	Profit or loss account	13261
	14059		14059

	£
Cash book figure	13102
Opening adjustment	-798
Closing adjustment	957
Motor vehicle expenses for the year ended 30/09/X7	13261

(d) (ii) Drag and drop the account names to the debit and credit columns to show the accounting entries for accrued motor expenses (reversal) at the beginning of the accounting period.

(3 marks)

The above ledger account working, showed the double entry for the accrued expenses (reversal) of £798 (a credit entry to motor vehicle expenses). The debit entry would be to accrued expenses (to reverse the liability in the statement of financial position at the beginning of the accounting period).

Debit
Accrued expenses

Credit
Motor vehicle expenses

Task 4 (23 marks)

The first tip with journal entries is to make sure all rows are completed in the exam task for example, 4 journal rows indicate that 4 entries will need to be completed.

The second tip is for the correction of suspense account errors. There are three different ways we can adjust for a suspense account error, so the number of rows included in the journal for correction of the error should help to guide you.

Three different ways to correct a suspense account error

- Adjust the error as a single adjustment between the suspense account and the incorrect account (2 rows). For example, if the bank had been credited correctly with £1,000 but motor vehicle expenses had been debited incorrectly with £900. Then debit motor vehicle expenses £100 and credit the suspense account £100.

- Reverse the whole amount of the error and correct the error for the whole amount, then bring any difference between these two entries as a single entry to the suspense account (3 rows). For example, if the bank had been credited correctly with £1,000 but motor vehicle expenses had been debited incorrectly with £900. Reverse the error by 'crediting' motor vehicle expenses with £900, correct the error by 'debiting' motor expenses with £1,000. The £100 'credit' remaining is posted to the suspense account to complete the double entry.

- Reverse the whole amount of the error and post the entry to the opposite side of the suspense account to complete the double entry. Correct the error for the whole amount and post the entry to the opposite side of the suspense account to complete the double entry (4 rows). For example, if the bank had been credited correctly with £1,000 but motor vehicle expenses had been debited incorrectly with £900. Reverse the error by 'crediting' motor vehicle expenses with £900 and debiting the suspense account with £900. Correct the error by 'debiting' motor vehicle expenses with £1,000 and crediting the suspense account with £1,000.

(a) Entries for prepaid rent expenses of £1,500 were made. The entries were on the correct side of both relevant general ledger accounts, but a figure of only £1,050 was incorrectly posted to prepaid expenses.

(6 marks)

Account	Dr £	Cr £
Prepaid expenses		1050
Suspense	1050	
Prepaid expenses	1500	
Suspense		1500

The double entry for prepaid expenses is DR prepaid expenses and CR rent expenses. Only £1,050 was debited to prepaid expenses. A suspense account would have therefore been opened to hold a difference for the £450 missing DR.

Reverse the whole amount of the error and post the entry to the opposite side of the suspense account to complete the double entry. Correct the error for the whole amount and post the entry to the opposite side of the suspense account to complete the double entry (4 rows).

The following workings may also help understand the logic.

	The task information		The Solution required		To help work out the solution	
Ledger account	HOW IT WAS		Journal		HOW IT SHOULD BE	
	Existing Balances				Revised Balances	
	Dr £	Cr £	Dr £	Cr £	Dr £	Cr £
Prepaid expenses	1050		1500	1050	1500	
Rent expenses		1500				1500
Suspense	450		1050	1500		
Total	1500	1500	2550	2550	1500	1500

(b) No entries have been made to the allowance for doubtful debts account. Allowance for doubtful debts needs to be 5% of trade receivables. Trade receivables for the year ended was £24,000.

(6 marks)

The allowance for doubtful debts is an account held in the financial position (always a credit balance) which offsets against the sales ledger control account (an asset) in the financial position (always a debit balance). The debit and credit balances offset to find the net amount owed by credit customers to the business.

The allowance for doubtful debts is calculated by applying a percentage expected doubtful debts against the SLCA (an asset) after accounting for any irrecoverable debts for the year-ended. In this question the SLCA is £24,000 and there is no irrecoverable debts.

The allowance for doubtful debts for the year end must be 5% of the SLCA £24,000. £24,000 ÷ 100% x 5% = £1,200. **DR £1,200 allowance for doubtful debts - adjustment (statement of profit or loss) as an expense and CR £1,200 allowance for doubtful debts (statement of financial position).**

Account	Dr £	Cr £
Allowance for doubtful debts – adjustment	1200	
Allowance for doubtful debts		1200

(c) A returned cheque by the bank of £840 from a credit customer was correctly entered into the bank account. No other entries were made.

(3 marks)

Account	Dr £	Cr £
SLCA	840	
Suspense		840

A dishonoured cheque needs to be credited to the bank account (since the original cash receipt would have been recorded as a debit to the bank account) and debited to the sales ledger control account (SLCA) to increase this asset balance.

£840 was entered correctly to the bank account (CR) but no other entry was made, the missing entry should have been made to the SLCA (DR). This single sided error has resulted in a suspense account balance of £840 debit.

The journal is 2 rows, so we need to make only 2 postings and one would definitely be the suspense account and the other as mentioned the SLCA.

The following workings may also help understand the logic.

	The task information		The Solution required		To help work out the solution	
	HOW IT WAS		Journal		HOW IT SHOULD BE	
Ledger account	Existing Balances				Revised Balances	
	Dr £	Cr £	Dr £	Cr £	Dr £	Cr £
Bank		840				840
SLCA			840		840	
Suspense	840			840		

(d) Premises repairs costing £720 were paid for by BACS. The correct amount was credited to the bank account and incorrectly debited to the buildings at cost account.

(3 marks)

Account	Dr £	Cr £
Buildings at cost		720
Premises expenses	720	

This error does not create an imbalance between DRs and CRs and a suspense account balance would not be required. The payment has gone to the wrong account, which was buildings at cost, so take it out of this incorrect account and post it to the correct account, which is premises expenses.

The following workings may also help understand the logic.

Ledger account	The task information		The Solution required		To help work out the solution	
	HOW IT WAS		Journal		HOW IT SHOULD BE	
	Existing Balances				Revised Balances	
	Dr £	Cr £	Dr £	Cr £	Dr £	Cr £
Bank		720				720
Buildings at cost	720			720		
Premises expenses			720		720	

(e) Which TWO of the following statements about suspense accounts are TRUE.

(2 marks)

used where a proper account cannot be determined at the time a transaction was recorded ✅

an account in the general ledger in which amounts are temporarily recorded ✅

indicates that the trial balance is free from errors and omissions ☐

should continue to appear in the general ledger for the business ☐

The suspense account is created due to errors or omissions that create an imbalance between debits and credits in the trial balance. But just because a trial balance does balance it does not guarantee the ledger accounts are free from errors and omissions. A suspense account is a temporary account until errors or omissions can be found and corrected.

(f) Identify which of the fundamental ethical principles is threatened if Barry continues to act for both companies. Choose ONE answer only.

(3 marks)

Answer a). objectivity and confidentiality. Objectivity because Barry has a conflict of interest, who is he representing and could he treat both parties fairly if in dispute? Confidentiality also because it would be very hard for Barry not to use the knowledge, he has for one Company if arguing the other's position. There is no indication Barry is acting dishonestly here (integrity) or showing any unprofessional behaviour such as breaking the rules. The last answer does include correctly confidentiality, but again no mention of Barry unable to do the tasks that he has been assigned to do (professional competence).

Task 5 (20 marks)

(a) What should Jim do to avoid being in breach of the fundamental ethical principles. Choose ONE answer.

(3 marks)

Answer C. Reject the offer of the gift and continue to review the clients records thoroughly. The acceptance of a gift could be perceived as bribery for Jim to keep quite about the issues he discovered in the financial statements, furthermore, for Jim to overlook the matter would breach many ethical principles including integrity, objectivity and professional behaviour.

(b) Use the following table to show the THREE adjustments that should appear in the sales ledger control account. Enter only ONE figure for each line. Do not enter zeros in unused cells.

(6 marks)

This task can examine adjustments to a sales ledger control account (SLCA), purchase ledger control account (PLCA) or the cash book from reconciliations already undertaken in the task.

Account	Dr £	Cr £
Adjustment 1		1100
Adjustment 3	34	
Adjustment 5		1280

1.	The total column of the sales daybook was overcast by £1,100. The amount posted to the sales ledger control account was £81,670, the correct amount that should have been posted is £80,570. **The total column of the sales daybook would be posted to the SLCA as a debit entry, sales invoices increasing the asset (money owed by customers). Overcast means 'over added' and £1,100 was debited too much to the SLCA.** CR SLCA £1,100 to correct the error.
2.	Sales returns of £1,220 have been credited to the sales ledger account of WX Traders Ltd instead of the sales ledger account of Mr Wren. **This does not effect the SLCA or the total balances in the sales ledger, as a customer account has been updated correctly, just the wrong customer account updated, so the sales ledger and SLCA would still agree.**
3.	A sales invoice of £34 for Strands Trading Ltd was omitted from the sales daybook. The correct entry was made in the sales ledger account of the customer. **Sales are a debit entry to the SLCA (increasing the asset, as more money owed by customers), if £34 missed from the sales daybook then it was not posted to the SLCA.** DR SLCA £34 to correct the error.
4.	A set-off entry of £504 was omitted from the sales ledger account of E. Barry. The correct entry was made in the sales ledger control account. **The balance of the customer account in the sales ledger needs reducing (credit entry) made of**

	£504. The total balances in the sales ledger will now fall by £504.
5.	Sales returns of £640 were in error debited to the sales ledger control account. The correct entry was made in the sales ledger account of the customer. **Sales returns should be a credit entry in the SLCA since this will reduce amounts outstanding by customers (the asset, money owed by customers is decreased). If £640 was debited in error, then we need to credit £640 to reverse the error, and then credit another £640 to post the correct entry. CR SLCA £1,280 to correct this error (CR £640 x 2 = CR £1,280).**
6.	An irrecoverable debt of £340 has been written off in the sales ledger control account. No entry was made in the sales ledger account of the customer. **The balance in customer account in the sales ledger needs reducing (credit entry) made of £340. The total balances in the sales ledger will now fall by £340.**

A SLCA showing the adjustments and the reconciliation (agreement) to the total balances in the sales ledger accounts has been shown below to aid logic and further understanding.

SLCA (Trade Receivables)

	£		£
Balance b/d	13042	Adjustment 1	1100
Adjustment 3	34	Adjustment 5	1280
		Balance c/d	10696
	13076		13076

Adjustments to sales ledger accounts

	£
Total balances from sales ledger accounts	11540
Adjustment 4	-504
Adjustment 6	-340
Revised (corrected) balance from SLCA	10696

Adjustment 2 is not a reconciling item and therefore ignored in the process above.

(c) Extend the figures into the columns for the statement of profit or loss and the statement of financial position. Do NOT enter zeros into unused column cells. Complete the extended trial balance by totalling the columns and entering any profit or loss figure for the year ended.

(11 marks)

Tutor note: the trial balance has two adjustments for closing inventory. The DR (an asset) for closing inventory to be included in the statement of financial position and a CR (reduction to purchases expenses) for closing inventory to be included within the statement of profit or loss for the year ended.

The exam will have autosum function for the trial balance totals, so you will not need to add up your columns in the exam task. There is also a picklist selection for the profit or loss for the year end which when the amount is included it should balance the last 4 columns of the ETB. If a loss for example below, then the loss amount is a credit to the statement of profit or loss (closing the profit or loss account for the year) and a debit (transfer) to the statement of financial position (decreasing the capital account balance owed to the owner of the business).

Ledger account	Ledger balances Dr £	Ledger balances Cr £	Adjustments Dr £	Adjustments Cr £	Statement of profit or loss Dr £	Statement of profit or loss Cr £	Statement of financial position Dr £	Statement of financial position Cr £
Bank		4103						4103
Opening inventory	8900				8900			
Prepayments			400				400	
Capital		11500						11500
Motor vehicle expenses	6722			1400	5322			
Staff wages	28039				28039			
Irrecoverable debts			6000		6000			
Depreciation charges			21508		21508			
Sales returns	1720			900	820			
Telephone expenses	1321			400	921			
Closing inventory			4300	4300		4300	4300	
VAT		3251						3251
Motor vehicle at cost	60050		1400				61450	
Motor vehicle accumulated depreciation		21017		21508				42525
Purchases	55430		1680		57110			
Purchase ledger control account		24591						24591
Sales		124000				124000		
Sales ledger control account	25500			6000			19500	
Suspense	780		900	1680				
Gross profit/loss for the year ⬍						320	320	
Total	188462	188462	36188	36188	128620	128620	85970	85970

Mock Exam Three
AAT L3 Advanced Book-keeping

Assessment information:

You have **2 hours** to complete this practice assessment.

This assessment contains **5 tasks** and you should attempt to complete **every** task.
Each task is independent. You will not need to refer to your answers to previous tasks.
Read every task carefully to make sure you understand what is required.

The standard rate of VAT is 20%.

Where the date is relevant, it is given in the task data.
Both minus signs and brackets can be used to indicate negative numbers **unless** task instructions say otherwise.

You must use a full stop to indicate a decimal point. For example, write 100.57 not 100,57 or 100 57
You may use a comma to indicate a number in the thousands, but you don't have to.
For example, 10000 and 10,000 are both acceptable.

Task 1 (21 marks)

This task is about non-current assets.

You are working on the accounting records of a business known as ABC Trading.

You may ignore VAT in this task.

The following is an extract from a purchase invoice received by ABC Trading relating to the purchase of new office equipment for its administration office.

To: ABC Trading	From: Z to B Stationers Invoice number: 023	Date: 1 April 20X9
Item	**Details**	**£**
Work Station Furniture (WSF)		950.00
2 office tables	@ £100 each	200.00
Printer		89.00
Printer paper		29.00
Net total		1556.00
Payment received by BACS.		

The following information relates to the sale by the business of its XCT Model Furniture which was replaced during the year.

Item description	XCT Model Furniture
Date of purchase	01/02/X7
Date of sale	24/04/X9
Cash sale	£500.00

ABC Trading has a policy of capitalising expenditure over £150.

- Computer equipment is depreciated over three years on a straight-line basis assuming no residual value.
- Office equipment is depreciated over five years on a straight-line basis assuming no residual value.
- A full year's depreciation is charged in the year of acquisition and none in the year of disposal.

(a) For the year ended 30 April 20X9, record the following in the extract from the non-current asset register of ABC Trading shown below.

- Any acquisitions of non-current assets
- Any disposals of non-current assets
- Depreciation

Note: Not every cell will require an entry and not all cells will accept entries. Choose answers where a grey picklist is given and insert figures into highlighted grey cells.
Show your numerical answers to TWO decimal places.
Use DD/MM/YY format for any dates.

(18 marks)

Description /Serial number	Acquisition date	Cost £	Depreciation charges £	Carrying amount £	Funding method	Disposal proceeds £	Disposal date
Office equipment							
XCT Model Furniture	01/02/X7	2000.00			Cash		
Year ended 30/04/X7			400.00	1600.00			
Year ended 30/04/X8			400.00	1200.00			
Year ended 30/04/X9							Picklist 1 ⬇
Picklist 3 ⬇	Picklist 2 ⬇				Picklist 4 ⬇		
Year ended 30/04/X9							
Computer equipment							
Model ZX PCs	22/08/X7	8400.00			Hire Purchase		
Year ended 30/04/X8			2800.00	5600.00			
Year ended 30/04/X9							
Model X PCs	06/04/X6	6500.00			Hire Purchase		
Year ended 30/04/X6			2166.67	4333.33			
Year ended 30/04/X7			2166.67	2166.67			
Year ended 30/04/X8			2166.67	0.00			
Year ended 30/04/X9							

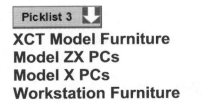

Picklist 1 ⬇	Picklist 2 ⬇	Picklist 3 ⬇	Picklist 4 ⬇
24/04/X9	06/04/X6	**XCT Model Furniture**	**Cash**
01/02/X7	22/08/X7	**Model ZX PCs**	**Finance Lease**
01/04/X9	01/02/X7	**Model X PCs**	**Hire Purchase**
30/04/X9	01/04/X9	**Workstation Furniture**	**Part Exchange**

A business needs to purchase a new van because the existing van is now much older and has become unreliable. The business has sufficient money in the bank account to help fund the purchase of new assets.

(b) Select the most suitable funding methods for acquisition of the new van. Select two options only from the list below.

(3 marks)

Funding Method	
Part Exchange	
Cash	
Finance Lease	
Bank Loan	

End of Task

Task 2 (17 marks)

This task is about ledger accounting for non-current assets.

You are working on the accounting records of a business for the year ended 30 September 20X9.

VAT can be ignored.

- A new car has been acquired at a cost of £28,950. The purchase was partly funded by a part-exchange value of £8,950, using an older car owned by the business. The remaining purchase price of the new car was funded by a bank loan.
- The business plans to sell the new car after 5 years when its residual value is expected to be £5,000.
- Motor vehicles are depreciated using the straight-line method. A full year's depreciation is charged in the year of acquisition and none in the year of disposal.
- Depreciation has already been entered below in the accounting records for existing cars but not for the new car purchased.
- The older car used as part-exchange originally cost £13,400 and had accumulated depreciation at the beginning of the accounting period of £7,500.

Make entries in the ledger accounts below for the acquisition and depreciation charge of the new car for the year ended 30 September 20X9. Make entries in the ledger accounts below for the disposal of the old car for the year ended 30 September 20X9. For each account show clearly the balance to be carried down or transferred to the statement of profit or loss, as appropriate.

(a) Make entries in the accounts below for:

- **The acquisition of the new vehicle**
- **The depreciation charge on the new vehicle**
- **The disposal of the old vehicle**

(13 marks)

Vehicles at cost

	£		£
Balance b/d	45900		
	45900		0

Vehicles accumulated depreciation

	£		£
		Balance b/d	19760
	0		19760

Depreciation charges

	£		£
Balance b/d	4500		
	4500		0

Disposals

	£		£
	0		0

A business purchased a computer on the 13 June 20X3 for £1,500. Computer equipment is depreciated at 40% per annum on a diminishing balance basis. Depreciation is calculated on an annual basis and charged in equal instalments for each full month the asset is owned for in each accounting period.

(b) For the year ended 31 May 20X5 complete the following calculations relating to the computer.

(4 marks)

(i) Calculate the depreciation charge for the computer to the nearest £

(ii) Calculate the carrying value of the computer to the nearest £

End of Task

Task 3 (19 marks)

This task is about accruals and prepayments, and ethical principles.

(a) Match the following statements in the table shown below to the correct fundamental ethical principles.

(3 marks)

Being discreet about whom disclosure of information can be made to.		⬇
To be honest, transparent and fair.		⬇
To comply with laws and regulations as a minimum requirement.		⬇

Picklist: Objectivity, Confidentiality, Professional competence and due care, Professional behaviour, Integrity.

You are working on the accounting records of a business for the year ended 30 June 20X4.

In this task, you can ignore VAT.

Business policy: accounting for accruals and prepayments
An entry is made to the income or expense account and an opposite entry to the relevant asset or liability account. In the following period, asset or liability entries are reversed.

You are looking at telephone expenses for the year.

- The cash book for the year shows payments for telephone expenses of £2,608.
- A telephone bill relating to the period 1 May 20X4 to 31 July 20X4 for £492 was not received until the 3 August 20X4 and is not included in the cash book for the year ended 30 June 20X4.

(b) Complete the following statement. Do NOT use a minus sign or brackets.

(4 marks)

The telephone expenses account needs an adjustment for

⬇	of	£		dated	⬇

Picklist
Prepaid expenses
Prepaid income
Accrued expenses
Accrued income

Picklist
30/06/X4
01/07/X3
01/07/X5
30/06/X5

(c) Update the telephone expenses account using the information in part (b).

Show clearly:

- **the cash book figure**
- **the year end adjustment**
- **the transfer to the statement of profit or loss for the year.** (6 marks)

Telephone expenses

	£		£
⬍		⬍	
⬍		⬍	
⬍		⬍	
	0		0

Picklist: Telephone expenses, Bank, Accrued expenses, Accrued income, Accrued income (reversal), Accrued expenses (reversal), Prepaid income, Statement of financial position, Prepaid income (reversal), Prepaid expenses (reversal), Profit or loss account, Prepaid expenses, Purchases ledger control account, Sales, Sales ledger control account, Balance b/d, Balance c/d.

The business has for rent expenses, a prepayment expenses reversal of £2,000 in its ledger accounts at the beginning of the accounting period.

(d) Complete the following tasks.

(4 marks)

(i) How are the elements of the accounting equation effected by this transaction. Tick ONE box for each row.

	Increase	Decrease	No change
Assets	☐	☐	☐
Liabilities	☐	☐	☐
Capital	☐	☐	☐

(ii) Which ONE of the following dates should be entered for this transaction in the ledger accounts of the business.

1 July 20X3	☐
30 June 20X4	☐
1 July 20X4	☐

(iii) Drag and drop the account names to the debit and credit columns to show the entries for the prepayment expenses (reversal) at the beginning of the accounting period.

(2 marks)

Prepaid expenses

Profit or loss account

Rent expenses

Debit	Credit

End of Task

This task is about accounting adjustments. You are working as an accounting technician on the accounting records of a business with a year ended of 30 April 20X7. A trial balance has been drawn up and a suspense account opened.

You now need to make some corrections and adjustments for the year ended.

You may ignore VAT in this task.

Record the journal entries required within the general ledger to deal with the items below.

You should:

- **remove any incorrect entries, as appropriate**
- **post the correct entries**

Note: You do NOT need to give narratives. Do NOT enter zeros into unused column cells.

> **Picklist for all journals below:** Purchases, Drawings, Capital, Motor vehicle expenses, Bank, Accrued expenses, Statement of financial position, Prepaid expenses, Irrecoverable debts, Motor vehicles at cost, Premises expenses, Profit or loss account, Purchases ledger control account, Sales ledger control account, Suspense, Closing inventory (financial position), Closing inventory (Profit or loss), Balance b/d, Balance c/d.

(a) No entries have been made for closing inventory for the year ended 30 April 20X7. Closing inventory has been valued at a cost of £27,320. Included in this amount is some inventory items costing £2,750 that can only be sold for £1,000.

(6 marks)

Account	Dr £	Cr £
⬇		
⬇		

(b) No entries were made for goods for resale that were taken by the owner of the business. The cost of the goods to the business was £3,000. No entries were made for a private motor vehicle valued at £7,000 that was transferred by the owner to the business.

(6 marks)

Account		Dr £	Cr £
	⇵		
	⇵		
	⇵		
	⇵		

(c) A payment of £187 for motor expenses was made by direct debit from the bank account. The correct entry was made in the bank account, no other entries were made.

(3 marks)

Account		Dr £	Cr £
	⇵		
	⇵		

(d) Motor vehicle repairs costing £720 were paid for by BACS. The correct amount was recorded, but the posting was in error debited to the bank account and credited to the motor vehicle expenses account.

(4 marks)

Account		Dr £	Cr £
	⇵		
	⇵		
	⇵		
	⇵		

You are working in practice as an accounting technician on the year-end accounts for clients. Your boss has called you into the office to delegate a task for you to complete. The task is regarding a technical accounting matter for a client's set of accounts, but you have very limited knowledge about this matter.

(e) Which ONE of the following statements would be an appropriate action to take. Choose ONE answer only.

(2 marks)

a) Behave with courtesy and consideration and carry on with the work assigned.
b) Do not accept or perform work unless you receive adequate advice and assistance to enable you to complete it.
c) Do not accept or perform the work as you are not competent and tell your boss this in no uncertain terms.

(f) Which ONE of the following statements is FALSE regarding irrecoverable debts expenses. Choose ONE answer only.

(2 marks)

a) It can be caused by customers obtaining goods and services prior to payment.
b) It is a loss that occurs when a customer does not pay their amounts owed.
c) It is a customer debt that is doubtful whether it will be collected.
d) It is written off from the customer sales ledger account and the sales ledger control account.

End of Task

Task 5 (20 marks)

This task is about period end routines, using accounting records, and the extended trial balance.

You are preparing a bank reconciliation for a business.

The balance showing on the bank statement is a credit of £4,197 and the balance in the cash book is a debit of £3,096.

The bank statement has been compared with the cash book for the year ended 31 July 20X3 and the following points have been noted.

1.	A cheque paid to a supplier during July 20X3 for £6,300 has not yet cleared the bank statements.
2.	Bank charges of £24 showing on the bank statements for the month July 20X3 have not been entered in the cash book.
3.	A remittance advice from a customer has been received and an entry made in the cash book for the correct amount of £3,400. This is not yet showing on the bank statements.
4.	The bank has made an error. A standing order payment for £508 which was correctly entered in the cash book has been duplicated on the bank statements.
5.	A supplier payment of £346 has been recorded in the cash book as a receipt.
6.	A cheque received from a credit customer for £575 has been dishonoured by the bank on the last day of the accounting period. No adjustment was made in the cash book.

(a) Use the following table to show the THREE adjustments that should be made as entries in the cash book. Enter only ONE figure for each line. Do not enter zeros in unused cells.

(6 marks)

Account	Dr £	Cr £
⬇		
⬇		
⬇		

Picklist: Item 1, Item 2, Item 3, Item 4, Item 5, Item 6.

(b) Which of the following statements would NOT be a benefit of using organisational policies and procedures. Choose ONE answer only.

(3 marks)

Ensures consistency for how things are dealt with by staff	☐
Gives instructions for staff to assist them to undertake their tasks	☐
Gives compliance and accountability to follow the rules	☐
Creates an inflexible and rigid framework for staff to do things	☐

You are now working on the accounting records of a different business.

You have the following extended trial balance. The adjustments have already been correctly entered.

(c) Extend the figures into the columns for the statement of profit or loss and the statement of financial position. Do NOT enter zeros into unused column cells. Complete the extended trial balance by totalling the columns and entering any profit or loss figure for the year ended.

(11 marks)

Extended trial balance

Ledger account	Ledger balances		Adjustments		Statement of profit or loss		Statement of financial position	
	Dr £	Cr £	Dr £	Cr £	Dr £	Cr £	Dr £	Cr £
Bank		7892						
Opening inventory	3000							
Accruals				542				
Capital		13089	6000					
Office stationery expenses	5671		542	600				
Payroll expenses	15600			6000				
Discounts received		450						
VAT		4522						
Prepayments			600					
Telephone expenses	1499							
Closing inventory			4500	4500				
Depreciation charges			3750					
Computers at cost	15000							
Computers accumulated depreciation		3750		3750				
Purchases	56733		4560					
Purchases ledger control		17800		4560				
Sales		65000						
Sales ledger control	13000							
Sales returns	2000							
⇩								
Total	112503	112503	19952	19952	Autosum	Autosum	Autosum	Autosum

> ⇩ **Picklist:** Profit/loss for the year, Suspense, Balance b/d, Balance c/d, Gross profit/loss for the year.

End of Task

Mock Exam Three
- Solutions
AAT L3 Advanced Book-keeping

You may find the following tutor notes useful when answering exam practice tasks.

Elements of the financial statements

Five elements make up the general ledger accounts and financial statements of a business.

Assets

A resource controlled by the business as a result of past events and from which future economic benefits (money) are expected to flow to the business.

- Premises, machines, motor vehicles, office equipment or furniture and fittings.
- Inventory currently for resale.
- Trade receivables (money to be 'received') also called sales ledger control account.
- Accrued income.
- Prepaid expenses.
- Money in the bank.
- Cash in hand.

Liabilities

A present obligation of the business arising from past events, the settlement of which is expected to result in an outflow from the business.

- VAT owed to HMRC
- Wages owed to staff
- Bank loans and overdrafts
- Trade payables (money to be 'paid') also called purchases ledger control account.
- Prepaid income.
- Accrued expenses.

Capital

The residual interest (whatever is left) from the assets of the business after deducting all of its liabilities. Total assets less total liabilities is equal to capital (also called 'net assets') of the business. This balance represents what is owed and accumulated by the business to its owner. A separate account for drawings can also be maintained in the general ledger, drawings is money taken from the business by the owner and rather than reducing the owners capital account for the money taken, a drawings account is kept as a separate account because it provides more information.

Income

Money earned or received by the business from the sale of goods or services that is makes or sells (its trade), or from other investments or trade sources.

- Cash sales (sales not on credit).
- Credit sales (sales on credit).
- Rent received from ownership and rental of premises.
- Bank interest received.
- Discounts received (PPD) from paying credit suppliers early.
- Commission received.

Expenses

Costs incurred or paid for by the business in the normal course of trade in order to earn income. The cost of goods sold and other expenses must be matched with the sales revenues earned in the same period.

- Cash purchases (inventory purchases for resale and not on credit).
- Credit purchases (inventory purchases for resale and on credit).
- Rent payments (if the business is renting a property).
- Staff wages
- Motor vehicle running costs.
- Advertising.
- Depreciation such as wear and tear or loss of value to long-term assets such as machines or motor vehicles.
- Bank interest and charges.
- Discounts allowed (PPD) to credit customers who pay early.
- Accountancy and legal services.
- Irrecoverable debts expense.
- Increase (debit)/Decrease (credit) in allowances for doubtful debts.

Income and expenses are used to work out the amount of profit the business has generated. Any profits are owed to the owner of the business and increase the capital account of the owner.

DEAD CLIC

Don't get clouded in the double entry logic, ledgers are balances kept for the five elements of the financial statements and we are increasing or decreasing these balances according to the rules of double entry.

Important double entry terminology

DEAD CLIC defines what is the 'normal balance' or the natural state for a T account (general, sales or purchase ledger account).

DEAD CLIC is an acronym which gives the elements of financial statements and whether each element would be a debit or credit balance overall within a double entry ledger system. It can be used for determining the correct debit or credit balance but the element must be determined first. It can also be used to determine the correct double entry to increase or decrease an account balance.

DEAD CLIC

Debit	Credit
Expenses	Liabilities
Assets	Income
Drawings	Capital

The elements	Natural state	Increase balance (as per the natural state)	Decrease balance (opposite to natural state)
Income	Credit	Credit	Debit
Expenses	Debit	Debit	Credit
Assets	Debit	Debit	Credit
Liabilities	Credit	Credit	Debit
Capital	Credit	Credit	Debit

Totalling and balancing ledger accounts

1. Look at both sides of the ledger account and find the side which has the biggest total amount (debits or credits).
2. Add up the 'total' of all the entries on the side that has the biggest total amount and put this 'total' amount on both sides of the ledger account.
3. Add up all the entries on the side of the ledger account that had the smallest total amount.
4. Work out on the side that had the smallest total amount, the difference between the total amount entered and the other entries made on this side. This is the balance carried down (c/d) at the end of the period.
5. The balance c/d is entered on the side of the ledger account that had the smallest total amount to ensure that both total amounts entered on either side of the ledger account agrees. This as an arithmetical control and considered good practice in manual ledger accounting.

The balance c/d is only a balancing figure to ensure both sides of the ledger account agree at the end of the period. The true debit or credit balance is brought down (b/d) on the opposite side to the balance carried down (c/d). The balance b/d is on the 1st (beginning) of the month and the balance c/d is at the end of the month 30th/31st (ignoring February).

The trial balance and errors

The purpose of a trial balance is to ensure that all entries made in an organisation's general ledger are properly balanced and to check the accuracy of entries made before a final set of financial accounts are produced. If the totals for debit and credit balances do not agree then errors have definitely occurred, but even if the totals for debit and credit balances do agree it does not guarantee the general ledger balances are free from errors or omissions.

Types of errors not disclosed by the trial balance

The following types of error all have one thing in common, the same amount has been debited and credited within the general ledger, but an error has still occurred. These type of errors do not cause an imbalance when a trial balance is prepared (total debits equal total credits in the trial balance). Types of errors not disclosed by the trial balance can be remembered using the acronym 'TOPCROC'. Because the trial balance will still balance these types of error are more difficult to detect.

- **T Transposition** (two or more digits are reversed when amounts are entered).
- **O Original entry** (errors occur when documents such as invoices or credit notes are prepared incorrectly or when erroneous documents are posted to the day books).
- **P Principle** (mis posting to the WRONG ledger account and WRONG financial element), for example an 'expense' debited instead to an 'asset', a fundamental error because assets and profits will be under or overstated.
- **C Commission** (mis posting to the WRONG ledger account but RIGHT financial element), for example an 'expense' debited instead to another type of 'expense', less fundamental than an error of principle because assets and profits will be not be under or overstated.
- **R Reversal of entries** (the debit and credit mis posted the wrong way around).
- **O Omission** of a transaction (no posting made in the general ledger).
- **C Compensating** errors (very rare but this can happen), two independent errors for two different amounts posted as a debit and credit, the two errors compensate and cancel each other out. The trial balance will still balance.

Types of errors disclosed by the trial balance

The following types of error all have one thing in common, they all cause an imbalance when a trial balance is prepared (total debits do not equal total credits in the trial balance). Types of errors disclosed by the trial balance can be remembered using the acronym 'TESCOS'.

- **T Transposition** e.g. error posted incorrectly on one side of a ledger account but correctly posted on the other side such as debit expenses £54 and credit bank £45.
- **E Extraction** e.g. a ledger balance is not totalled and balanced correctly, so the wrong ledger balance is now 'extracted' and represented incorrectly in the trial balance.
- **S Single entry** e.g. a debit entry posted, but no credit entry posted, or vice versa.
- **C Casting** (casting means 'adding') e.g. a column in a day book casted (added up) incorrectly and the incorrect amount posted to the general ledger.
- **O Omission** of a ledger balance within the trial balance e.g. a ledger balance completely missed out and not included in the trial balance.
- **S Same sided** e.g. 2 debit entries only posted in error, or 2 credit entries only posted in error, rather than a debit and a credit entry made correctly.

Examples of how suspense accounts are opened

Example 1

Trial Balance (totals before suspense account opened)	154,896	155,279
Suspense account opened (debit balance)	383	
Trial balance totals agree until error(s) found	155,279	155,279

Example 1 the trial balance does not balance. The suspense account is always opened for the difference that exists between debits and credits and to ensure debits equal credits. The larger amount is credit £155,279 and the smaller amount is debit £154,896. A debit amount of £155,279 - £154,896 = £383 is missing. A suspense account is opened as £383 debit balance to ensure the trial balance agrees and until the error(s) has been found.

Example 2

Trial Balance (totals before suspense account opened)	121,780	99,800
Suspense account opened (credit balance)		21,980
Trial balance totals agree until error(s) found	121,780	121,780

Example 2 the trial balance does not balance. The larger amount is debit £121,780 and the smaller amount is credit £99,800. A credit amount of £121,780 - £99,800 = £21,980 is missing. A suspense account is opened as £21,980 credit balance to ensure the trial balance agrees and until the error(s) has been found.

Task 1 (21 marks)

Part (a) (18 marks)

Description /Serial number	Acquisition date	Cost £	Depreciation charges £	Carrying amount £	Funding method	Disposal proceeds £	Disposal date
Office equipment							
XCT Model Furniture	01/02/X7	2000.00			Cash		
Year ended 30/04/X7			400.00	1600.00			
Year ended 30/04/X8			400.00	1200.00			
Year ended 30/04/X9			0.00	0.00		500.00	24/04/X9
Workstation Furniture	**01/04/X9**	**950.00**			**Cash**		
Year ended 30/04/X9			190.00	760.00			
Computer equipment							
Model ZX PCs	22/08/X7	8400.00			Hire Purchase		
Year ended 30/04/X8			2800.00	5600.00			
Year ended 30/04/X9			2800.00	2800.00			
Model X PCs	06/04/X6	6600.00			Hire Purchase		
Year ended 30/04/X6			2200.00	4400.00			
Year ended 30/04/X7			2200.00	2200.00			
Year ended 30/04/X8			2200.00	0.00			
Year ended 30/04/X9			0.00	0.00			

XCT Model Furniture (sold)

- The XCT Model Furniture would be removed from the accounting records of the business by posting both the cost and accumulated depreciation of this asset to a disposal account. The carrying value would always be zero in the non-current asset register because the asset has been removed from the books of the business.
- No depreciation on this asset for the year-ended due to the policy of the business of none charged in the year of disposal.
- The correct date of sale (disposal) and the disposal proceeds amount from sale are also required to be entered in the non-current asset register.

Workstation Furniture and other items purchased

To: ABC Trading	From: Z to B Stationers Invoice number: 023	Date: 1 April 20X9
Item	**Details**	**£**
Workstation Furniture (WSF)		**950.00**
2 office tables	@ £100 each	200.00
Printer		89.00
Printer paper		29.00
Net total		1556.00
Payment received by BACS.		

Capitalisation of cost for the new furniture

- £950 is capital expenditure.

- The 2 office tables are '£100 each' and each below the £150 threshold of the accounting policy for capitalising expenditure. There is no indication the items are purchased as a 'set' along with the Workstation Furniture (WSF). These items would not be capitalised and instead written off as revenue expenses.

When purchasing an asset, the invoice may state individually the cost of separate items together which make up the whole or 'aggregate' of an asset. For example, the Workstation Furniture (WSF) and 2 office tables could have been purchased as a 'furniture set' and made up of individual items which are separately charged for, but there is no indication of this from the information given. If alternatively, a dining room table and 6 chairs for the dining room table were purchased as a 'dining room set' then the individual items in particular the chairs, even if below the materiality threshold, would be aggregated with the cost of the table and all the expenditure capitalised.

- The printer is £89 and below the £150 threshold. Like the office tables it would not be capitalised and instead written off as revenue expenses.

- Printer paper is revenue not capital expenditure, since the benefit of paper is normally consumed by the business within one year. Unlike capital expenditure which is money spent by a business to acquire 'non-current assets' which are normally used within the business and consumed beyond a 12-month period.

- The total cost that should be capitalised (items highlighted red bold in the invoice above) would the £950.00 only.

Depreciation for the Workstation Furniture (WSF)

- Office equipment is depreciated over five years on a straight-line basis assuming no residual value.
- £950 is capitalised with no residual value ÷ 5 years = £190 depreciation per year. A full year's depreciation is charged in the year of acquisition.
- The carrying value at the year end would be £950 - £190 = £760.

Model ZX PCs

- Computer equipment is depreciated over three years on a straight-line basis assuming no residual value.
- £8400.00 original cost and no residual value ÷ 3 years = £2800.00 depreciation per annum.
- The carrying value at the year-end would be £5600.00 carrying value at the beginning of the year - £2800.00 depreciation during the year = £2800.00.

Model X PCs

- This computer equipment is fully depreciated from previous accounting periods.
- The carrying value at the beginning of the accounting period was 0.00. So, at the end of this accounting period it would be the same. The asset has not been sold and therefore details remain on the non-current asset register.
- No depreciation is charged since the asset has been fully depreciated.

Part (b) (3 marks)

Given the business has cash available and an old van it wants to dispose of the best two options would be **cash** and **part exchange**.

Task 2 (17 marks)

(a) Make entries in the accounts below for:

- **The acquisition of the new vehicle**
- **The depreciation charge on the new vehicle**
- **The disposal of the old vehicle**

(13 marks)

Depreciation on the new car

The straight-line method uses a constant amount of depreciation each year:

Straight Line Depreciation per annum = (Cost - Residual Value) / Useful Life.

Straight Line Depreciation per annum = (£28,950 - £5,000) / 5 years = £4,790. A full year's depreciation is charged in the year of acquisition.

Vehicles at cost

	£		£
Balance b/d	45900	Disposals	13400
Bank loan	20000	Balance c/d	61450
Disposals	8950		
	74850		74850

Vehicles accumulated depreciation

	£		£
Disposals	7500	Balance b/d	19760
Balance c/d	17050	Depreciation charges	4790
	24550		24550

Depreciation charges

	£		£
Balance b/d	4500	Profit or loss account	9290
Vehicles accumulated depreciation	4790		
	9290		9290

Disposals

	£		£
Vehicles at cost	13400	Vehicles accumulated depreciation	7500
Profit or loss account	3050	Vehicles at cost	8950
	16450		16450

(b) For the year ended 31 May 20X5 complete the following calculations relating to the computer.

(4 marks)

(i) Calculate the depreciation charge for the computer to the nearest £380.

(ii) Calculate the carrying value of the computer to the nearest £570.

Depreciation is calculated on an annual basis and charged in equal instalments for each full month the asset is owned for in each accounting period.

- **Year ended 31 May 20X4** (year of purchase) the computer had been owned for the period 13/06/X3 to 31/05/X4, which was for 11 full months. Depreciation for the year would be £1,500 x 40% = £600. Given we need 11 months depreciation, £600 ÷ 12 months = £50 per month x 11 months = £550. Given you multiply by 11 and divide by 12 then a quicker calculation using fractions would be £600 x 11/12 = £550.
- The carrying value would be £1,500 cost - £550 depreciation charges = £950.

- **Year ended 31 May 20X5** the computer had been owned for a full year in this accounting period. The carrying value is now £950. Depreciation for this year would be £950 x 40% = £380 depreciation charged for the computer.
- The carrying value would now be £950 carrying value at the beginning of the year - £380 depreciation charges in the year = £570.

Task 3 (19 marks)

This task is about accruals and prepayments, and ethical principles.

(a) Match the following statements in the table shown below to the correct fundamental ethical principles.

(3 marks)

Being discreet about whom disclosure of information can be made to.	Confidentiality
To be honest, transparent and fair.	Integrity
To comply with laws and regulations as a minimum requirement.	Professional behaviour

(b) Complete the following statement. Do NOT use a minus sign or brackets.

(4 marks)

The telephone expenses account needs an adjustment for

Accrued expenses ⬇   of   £ 328   dated 30/06/X4 ⬇

A telephone bill relating to the period 1 May 20X4 to 31 July 20X4 for £492 was not received until the 3 August 20X4 and is not included in the cash book for the year ended 30 June 20X4.

The year end of the business is 30 June 20X4 and 2 months of the telephone bill relates to the year end of the business, the period 1 May 20X4 to 30 June 20X4. The period 1 July 20X4 to 31 July 20X4 is ignored because this expense relates to the next accounting period.

We need to pro rate the three-month bill on a monthly (average) basis to find an amount for two months that relates to a three month period. £492 ÷ 3 months = £164 per month (average) x 2 months = £328 accrued telephone expenses. £328 of telephone expenses that have been consumed by the business but not recognised in the books of the business for the year-ended 30 June 20X4.

The entry is always recorded in the ledger system on the last day of the accounting period which would be 30 June 20X4.

(c) Update the telephone expenses account using the information in part (b).

Show clearly:

- **the cash book figure**
- **the year end adjustment**
- **the transfer to the statement of profit or loss for the year.**

(6 marks)

Telephone expenses

	£		£
Bank	2608	Profit and loss account	2936
Accrued expenses	328		
	2936		2936

Accrued expenses are a liability, the business owes for telephone expenses consumed in the accounting period but not paid for, so a credit entry of £328 would be made to this account to increase liabilities. The debit entry would be made to telephone expenses, increasing expenses by £328 which have been consumed and recognised in this accounting period.

(d) Complete the following tasks.

(4 marks)

(i) How are the elements of the accounting equation effected by this transaction. Tick ONE box for each row.

The business has for rent expenses, a prepayment expenses reversal of £2,000 in its ledger accounts at the beginning of the accounting period.

A prepaid expense is an expense paid for but the benefit not consumed (used) by the business in the accounting year. It is an asset, so debit prepaid expenses (increase assets) and a reduce (credit) expenses charged for the year. A prepayment expenses (reversal) would simply be the opposite to the double entry required at the beginning of the accounting period.

A prepaid expense (reversal) would be debit expenses (rent expenses) and credit assets (prepaid expenses). The effect on the accounting equation is to reduce (credit) assets and increase (debit) expenses, if expenses go up then profits will go down and the capital account of the owner would go down because less profit is earned.

	Increase	Decrease	No change
Assets	☐	✓	☐
Liabilities	☐	☐	✓
Capital	☐	✓	☐

(ii) Which ONE of the following dates should be entered for this transaction in the ledger accounts of the business.

1 July 20X3	☑
30 June 20X4	☐
1 July 20X4	☐

The 'reversal' of accruals and prepayments are always entries made in the ledger accounts on the first day of the accounting period. This business has a year end of 30 June 20X4, the beginning of the accounting period would be 1 July 20X3.

(iii) Drag and drop the account names to the debit and credit columns to show the entries for the prepayment expenses (reversal) at the beginning of the accounting period.

(2 marks)

A prepaid expense (reversal) would be debit expenses (rent expenses) and credit assets (prepaid expenses).

Debit
Rent expenses

Credit
Prepaid expenses

Task 4 (23 marks)

The first tip with journal entries is to make sure all rows are completed in the exam task for example, 4 journal rows indicate that 4 entries will need to be completed.

The second tip is for the correction of suspense account errors. There are three different ways we can adjust for a suspense account error, so the number of rows included in the journal for correction of the error should help to guide you.

Three different ways to correct a suspense account error

- Adjust the error as a single adjustment between the suspense account and the incorrect account (2 rows). For example, if the bank had been credited correctly with £1,000 but motor vehicle expenses had been debited incorrectly with £900. Then debit motor vehicle expenses £100 and credit the suspense account £100.

- Reverse the whole amount of the error and correct the error for the whole amount, then bring any difference between these two entries as a single entry to the suspense account (3 rows). For example, if the bank had been credited correctly with £1,000 but motor vehicle expenses had been debited incorrectly with £900. Reverse the error by 'crediting' motor vehicle expenses with £900, correct the error by 'debiting' motor expenses with £1,000. The £100 'credit' remaining is posted to the suspense account to complete the double entry.

- Reverse the whole amount of the error and post the entry to the opposite side of the suspense account to complete the double entry. Correct the error for the whole amount and post the entry to the opposite side of the suspense account to complete the double entry (4 rows). For example, if the bank had been credited correctly with £1,000 but motor vehicle expenses had been debited incorrectly with £900. Reverse the error by 'crediting' motor vehicle expenses with £900 and debiting the suspense account with £900. Correct the error by 'debiting' motor vehicle expenses with £1,000 and crediting the suspense account with £1,000.

(a) No entries have been made for closing inventory for the year ended 30 April 20X7. Closing inventory has been valued at a cost of £27,320. Included in this amount is some inventory items costing £2,750 that can only be sold for £1,000.

(6 marks)

Account	Dr £	Cr £
Closing inventory (profit and loss)		25570
Closing inventory (financial position)	25570	

Inventory is an asset (goods held for resale) and should be valued at the lower of purchase cost or net realisable value (NRV). NRV means what the inventory can be sold (after any further costs of sale). £27,320 includes £2,750 that can be sold for only £1,000 NRV. £27,320 - £2,750 + £1,000 = £25,570 closing inventory value.

As a period end adjustment closing inventory is presented as an asset in the statement of financial position (goods held for resale), a debit entry to increase assets. Also a reduction in cost of sales in the statement of profit and loss account, a credit entry to reduce expenses.

(b) No entries were made for goods for resale that were taken by the owner of the business. The cost of the goods to the business was £3,000. No entries were made for a private motor vehicle valued at £7,000 that was transferred by the owner to the business.

(6 marks)

Personal goods taken by the owner for personal use must be removed from purchase expenses for the year (CR purchases to reduce this expenses) and posted to drawings (DR drawings) which records goods taken by the owner. Drawings is a debit balance and represents money or goods taken by the owner from the business, it is offset against the capital account (a credit balance) of the owner.

When the owner pays in money or transfers personal assets into the business then CR capital (the credit increasing the amount owed to the owner by the business) and DR the asset in this case a motor vehicle.

Account	Dr £	Cr £
Drawings	3000	
Purchases		3000
Motor vehicles at cost	7000	
Capital		7000

(c) A payment of £187 for motor expenses was made by direct debit from the bank account. The correct entry was made in the bank account, no other entries were made.

(3 marks)

A payment has been credited to the bank account but no other entry to motor expenses was been made (which would be a debit entry). A suspense account balance for a debit amount of £187 would be created due to this error.

The journal is 2 rows, so we need to post (DR) motor expenses with £187 to correct the omission and reverse the entry made in the suspense account (CR £187).

Account	Dr £	Cr £
Motor vehicle expenses	187	
Suspense		187

The following workings may also help understand the logic.

Ledger account	The task information		The Solution required		To help work out the solution	
	HOW IT WAS		Journal		HOW IT SHOULD BE	
	Existing Balances				Revised Balances	
	Dr £	Cr £	Dr £	Cr £	Dr £	Cr £
Bank		187				187
Motor vehicle expenses			187		187	
Suspense	187			187		
Total	187	187	187	187	187	187

(d) Motor vehicle repairs costing £720 were paid for by BACS. The correct amount was recorded, but the posting was in error debited to the bank account and credited to the motor vehicle expenses account.

(4 marks)

The entry was for the payment of expenses DR Expenses and CR Bank. In this case the entry in error was made in reverse. We need to reverse the incorrect entry and then record the correct entry in the journal as 4 rows exist to make the correction. No suspense account would be created from this error since the posting was in reverse but a DR and CR for equal amounts was made.

Account	Dr £	Cr £
Motor vehicle expenses	720	
Bank		720
Motor vehicle expenses	720	
Bank		720

(e) Which ONE of the following statements would be an appropriate action to take. Choose ONE answer only.

(2 marks)

Answer (b). Do not accept or perform work unless you receive adequate advice and assistance to enable you to complete it.

The ethical principle of professional competence and due care means you must not accept or perform work that you are not competent to undertake unless you receive adequate advice and assistance to enable you to complete it competently. You also need to maintain professional standards expected from you. You have very limited knowledge in the scenario so should not just carry on with the work assigned. To refuse entirely could be seen as unprofessional behaviour.

(f) Which ONE of the following statements is FALSE regarding irrecoverable debts expenses. Choose ONE answer only.

(2 marks)

All statements about irrecoverable debts are correct except **answer (c)**. If a customer debt is doubtful whether it will be collected, this is more an explanation of a doubtful debt allowance rather than an irrecoverable debt.

Task 5 (20 marks)

Part (a) 6 marks

This task can examine adjustments to a sales ledger control account (SLCA), purchase ledger control account (PLCA) or the cash book from reconciliations already undertaken in the task.

Account	Dr £	Cr £
Item 2		24
Item 5		692
Item 6		575

1.	A cheque paid to a supplier during July 20X3 for £6,300 has not yet cleared the bank statements. **This is a timing difference on the bank statement as the payment has yet to clear, no adjustment to the cash book is required.**
2.	Bank charges of £24 showing on the bank statements for the month July 20X3 have not been entered in the cash book. **The omitted item needs to be entered as a payment in the cash book. CR Cash Book £24.**
3.	A remittance advice from a customer has been received and an entry made in the cash book for the correct amount of £3,400. This is not yet showing on the bank statements. **This is a timing difference on the bank statement as the outstanding lodgement (money paid in) has yet to clear, no adjustment to the cash book is required.**
4.	The bank has made an error. A standing order payment for £508 which was correctly entered in the cash book has been duplicated on the bank statements. **This is not an error in the cash book but you would have to adjust the bank balance on the bank statements if a bank reconciliation was performed.**
5.	A supplier payment of £346 has been recorded in the cash book as a receipt. **A payment should be a credit entry not a debit entry in the cash book. The £346 payment has been debited in error, we need to credit £346 to the cash book to cancel the error and then credit another £346 to post the correct entry. CR Cash Book £692 (2 x £346).**
6.	A cheque received from a credit customer for £575 has been dishonoured by the bank on the last day of the accounting period. No adjustment was made in the cash book. **A receipt from a customer would be a debit to the cash book and a credit to the SLCA. The cheque from the customer has been returned so reverse the original entry to cancel this out. CR Cash Book £575.**

A cash book showing the adjustments and the bank reconciliation (agreement) has been shown below to aid logic and further understanding.

Bank

	£		£
Balance b/d	3096	Item 2	24
		Item 5	692
		Item 6	575
		Balance c/d	1805
	3096		3096

Bank reconciliation

	£
Balance as per bank statement	4197
Item 1	-6300
Item 3	3400
Item 4	508
Revised (corrected) bank balance	1805

Part (b) 3 marks

Ensures consistency for how things are dealt with by staff	☐
Gives instructions for staff to assist them to undertake their tasks	☐
Gives compliance and accountability to follow the rules	☐
Creates an inflexible and rigid framework for staff to do things	☑

Creating an inflexible and rigid framework for staff to do things, makes it difficult to implement change. This would not be a benefit. All other statements provided are benefits of having organisational policies and procedures.

Part (c) 11 marks

(c) Extend the figures into the columns for the statement of profit or loss and the statement of financial position. Do NOT enter zeros into unused column cells. Complete the extended trial balance by totalling the columns and entering any profit or loss figure for the year ended.

(11 marks)

Tutor note: the trial balance has two adjustments for closing inventory. The DR (an asset) for closing inventory to be included in the statement of financial position and a CR (reduction to purchases expenses) for closing inventory to be included within the statement of profit or loss for the year ended.

The exam will have autosum function for the trial balance totals, so you will not need to add up your columns in the exam task. There is also a picklist selection for the profit or loss for the year end which when the amount is included it should balance the last 4 columns of the ETB. If a loss for example below, then the loss amount is a credit to the statement of profit or loss (closing the profit or loss account for the year) and a debit (transfer) to the statement of financial position (decreasing the capital account balance owed to the owner of the business).

Ledger account	Ledger balances		Adjustments		Statement of profit or loss		Statement of financial position	
	Dr £	Cr £	Dr £	Cr £	Dr £	Cr £	Dr £	Cr £
Bank		7892						7892
Opening inventory	3000				3000			
Accruals				542				542
Capital		13089	6000					7089
Office stationery expenses	5671		542	600	5613			
Payroll expenses	15600			6000	9600			
Discounts received		450				450		
VAT		4522						4522
Prepayments			600				600	
Telephone expenses	1499				1499			
Closing inventory			4500	4500		4500	4500	
Depreciation charges			3750		3750			
Computers at cost	15000						15000	
Computers accumulated depreciation		3750		3750				7500
Purchases	56733			4560	61293			
Purchases ledger control		17800		4560				22360
Sales		65000				65000		
Sales ledger control	13000						13000	
Sales returns	2000				2000			
Gross profit/loss for the year ⊔						16805	16805	
Total	112503	112503	19952	19952	86755	86755	49905	49905

Mock Exam Four
AAT L3 Advanced Book-keeping

Assessment information:

You have **2 hours** to complete this practice assessment.

This assessment contains **5 tasks** and you should attempt to complete **every** task.
Each task is independent. You will not need to refer to your answers to previous tasks.
Read every task carefully to make sure you understand what is required.

The standard rate of VAT is 20%.

Where the date is relevant, it is given in the task data.
Both minus signs and brackets can be used to indicate negative numbers **unless** task instructions say otherwise.

You must use a full stop to indicate a decimal point. For example, write 100.57 not 100,57 or 100 57
You may use a comma to indicate a number in the thousands, but you don't have to.
For example, 10000 and 10,000 are both acceptable.

Task 1 (21 marks)

This task is about non-current assets.

You are working on the accounting records of a business known as ABC Warehouse.

ABC Warehouse is a VAT registered business.

The business purchased a new van during the accounting period.   The relevant purchase invoice is shown below.

To: ABC Warehouse	**From:** INDU Suppliers Invoice number: 001239	**Date:** 7 October 20X7
Item	**Details**	**£**
Forklift INDUX		19,950.00
Weatherproof cover	for Forklift INDUX	550.00
Recharging kits for INDUX forklift	@ £144.50 each	289.00
Delivery		100.00
Net total		20,889.00
VAT 20%		4,177.80
Total		25,066.80
Hire purchase arrangement 17.6% interest rate per annum.		

VAT can be reclaimed on the purchase of the items above.

The following relates to a forklift truck which was sold by the business during the year.

Item description	Forklift TKO
Date of purchase	04/02/X7
Date of sale	24/03/X8
Cash sale	£3,400.00 plus VAT

ABC Warehouse has a policy of capitalising expenditure over £500.

- Plant and machinery is depreciated at 30% per annum on a diminishing balance basis.
- Computer equipment is depreciated at 40% per annum on a diminishing balance basis.
- Industrial fixtures are depreciated over ten years on a straight-line basis assuming no residual value.
- Depreciation is calculated on an annual basis and charged in equal instalments for each full month the asset is owned in the year.

(a) For the year ended 31 March 20X8, record the following in the extract from the non-current asset register of ABC Warehouse shown below.

- Any acquisitions of non-current assets
- Any disposals of non-current assets
- Depreciation charges

Note: Not every cell will require an entry and not all cells will accept entries. Choose answers where a grey picklist is given and insert figures into highlighted grey cells.
Show your numerical answers to TWO decimal places.
Use DD/MM/YY format for any dates.

(18 marks)

Description /Serial number	Acquisition date	Cost £	Depreciation charges £	Carrying amount £	Funding method	Disposal proceeds £	Disposal date
Plant and equipment							
Forklift TKO	04/02/X7	15500.00			Hire Purchase		
Year ended 30/09/X7			2712.50	12787.50			
Year ended 30/09/X8							Picklist 1 ⬇
Picklist 3 ⬇	Picklist 2 ⬇				Picklist 4 ⬇		
Year ended 30/09/X8							
Computer equipment							
Warehouse PCs	01/10/X5	8400.00			Bank Loan		
Year ended 30/09/X6			3360.00	5040.00			
Year ended 30/09/X7			2016.00	3024.00			
Year ended 30/09/X8							
Industrial fixtures							
Warehouse shelving	06/08/X6	25000.00			Bank Loan		
Year ended 30/09/X6			208.33	24791.67			
Year ended 30/09/X7			2500.00	22291.67			
Year ended 30/09/X8							

Picklist 1 ⬇	Picklist 2 ⬇	Picklist 3 ⬇	Picklist 4 ⬇
06/08/X6	24/03/X8	Forklift TKO	Cash
24/03/X8	04/02/X7	Warehouse PCs	Finance Lease
04/02/X7	06/08/X6	Warehouse shelving	Hire Purchase
07/10/X7	07/10/X7	Forklift INDUX	Loan

(b) Complete the following multiple-choice question. (3 marks)

Non-current assets are generally high value items that can be used in the business for many years. It is important that policies and procedures exist to handle the way that non-current assets are approved and funded. Which one of the following organisational policies and procedures is more likely used for the approval of capital expenditure.

    a) Authorisation limits.
    b) Materiality limits for record keeping.
    c) Non-current asset registers.
    d) Regular physical inspection of assets for wear and tear, or obsolescence.

End of Task

Task 2 (17 marks)

This task is about ledger accounting for non-current assets.

You are working on the accounting records of a business for the year ended 30 April 20X3.

VAT can be ignored in this task.

- Computer equipment was sold on 12 December 20X2 and the sale proceeds of £1,500 was paid into the bank account. This computer equipment had originally cost £9,200 and had accumulated depreciation of £4,722.
- New computer equipment was purchased for £8,400 and was paid for from the bank account on 23 November 20X2.
- Computer equipment is depreciated at 30% per annum on a diminishing balance basis. A full year's depreciation is charged in the year of acquisition and none in the year of disposal.
- The original cost and depreciation has already been entered in the accounting records shown below for existing computer equipment, but does not include entries for the new computer equipment.

Make entries in the accounts below for the acquisition and depreciation charge for the new computer equipment for the year ended 30 April 20X3. Make entries in the accounts below for the disposal of the old computer equipment for the year ended 30 April 20X3. For each account show clearly the balance to be carried down or transferred to the statement of profit or loss, as appropriate.

(a) (i) Make entries in the accounts below for:

- **The acquisition of the new computer equipment**
- **The depreciation charge on the new computer equipment**
- **The disposal of the old computer equipment**

(11 marks)

Picklist: Bank, Depreciation charges, Disposals, Computers accumulated depreciation, Computers at cost, Profit or loss account, Purchases, Stationary, Purchases ledger control account, Sales, Sales ledger control account, Bank loan, Computers running expenses. Balance b/d, Balance c/d.

Computers at cost

	£			£
Balance b/d	9200		⬍	
⬍			⬍	
⬍			⬍	
	9200			0

Computers accumulated depreciation

	£			£
⬍		Balance b/d		4722
⬍			⬍	
⬍			⬍	
	0			4722

Depreciation charges

	£			£
⬍			⬍	
⬍			⬍	
⬍			⬍	
	0			0

Disposals

	£			£
⬍			⬍	
⬍			⬍	
⬍			⬍	
	0			0

(a) (ii) Complete the following sentence.

A gain was earned from the disposal of the old computer equipment.
(Select: TRUE **or** FALSE**)**

(1 mark)

A crude oil processing plant originally cost £12 million and has an estimated capacity to process 50 million barrels of crude oil during its useful life. Production during the first year of operation was 2 million barrels.

The expected residual value of the processing plant when sold at the end of its useful life is £2 million. The oil company applies the units of production method as its depreciation method.

(b) For the year ended complete the following calculations relating to the processing plant for its first year of operation. Round each answer to one decimal place.

(5 marks)

(i) Calculate the depreciation charge for the plants first year of operation.

£ [   ]

(ii) Calculate the carrying value at the end of the first year.

£ [   ]

- -

End of Task

Task 3 (19 marks)

This task is about ledger accounting, including accruals and prepayments, and ethical principles.

You are working on the accounting records of a business for the year ended 31 March 20X5.

In this task you should ignore VAT.

Business policy: accounting for accruals and prepayments
An entry is made to the income or expense account and an opposite entry to the relevant asset or liability account. In the following period, asset or liability entries are reversed.

You are looking at interest received as income for the year.

- The cash book for the year shows receipts for interest income of £360.
- The £360 does not include £120 of interest earned for the period 01/03/X5 to 31/05/X5. This was credited in the bank statements on 02/06/X5.

(a) Update the interest income account.

Show clearly:

- **the cash book figure**
- **the year end adjustment**
- **the transfer to the statement of profit or loss for the year.**   (6 marks)

Interest income

	£			£
Accrued income (reversal)	80		⮂	
⮂			⮂	
⮂			⮂	
	80			0

Picklist: Interest expenses, Interest income, Bank, Accrued expenses, Accrued income, Accrued income (reversal), Accrued expenses (reversal), Prepaid income, Statement of financial position, Prepaid income (reversal), Prepaid expenses (reversal), Profit or loss account, Prepaid expenses, Purchases ledger control account, Sales, Sales ledger control account, Balance b/d, Balance c/d.

(b) Answer the following regarding the accrued income (reversal) of £80 in (a) above.

(4 marks)

(i) How are the elements of the accounting equation effected by this transaction. Tick ONE box for each row.

	Increase	Decrease	No change
Assets	☐	☐	☐
Liabilities	☐	☐	☐
Capital	☐	☐	☐

(ii) Which ONE of the following dates should be entered for this transaction in the ledger account shown in (a) above.

31 March 20X5	☐
1 April 20X5	☐
1 April 20X4	☐

The business paid during the accounting period £3,042 of electricity expenses and had accrued electricity expenses of £352 for the year ended 31 March 20X5. There was also an accrued expenses reversal for electricity expenses at the beginning of the accounting period of £498.

(c) (i) Calculate electricity expenses for the year ended 31 March 20X5 and complete the table shown below. If necessary, use a minus sign to indicate ONLY the deduction of an amount from the cash book figure.

(3 marks)

	£
Cash book figure	
Opening adjustment	
Closing adjustment	
Electricity expenses for the year ended 31/03/X5	

(c) (ii) Drag and drop the account names to the debit and credit columns to show the entries for providing for accrued expenses of £352 for the year end 31 March 20X5.

(3 marks)

Accrued expenses
Electricity expenses
Profit or loss account

Debit	Credit

Jacob works as an accountant in practice. Jacob is conducting a second interview for an excellent candidate (an AAT student) for a junior post in Jacob's tax department.

When discussing remuneration, the potential employee stated that she will bring a copy of the database of clients from her old firm to introduce new clients to Jacob's business. She stated that she knows a lot of negative information about her old firm which Jacob could use to gain clients from them.

(d) Which ONE of the following is the least likely action that Jacob should take following this interview.

(3 marks)

a) She shows good business acumen and promise, offer her the job.
b) She has breached the fundamental principles of integrity and confidentiality, report her to the AAT.
c) She lacks integrity, inform her that she will not be offered the job.

End of Task

Task 4 (23 marks)

This task is about accounting adjustments. You are working as an accounting technician on the accounting records of a business for the year ended 30 June 20X7. A trial balance has been drawn up and a suspense account opened.

You now need to make some corrections and adjustments for the year ended.

You may ignore VAT in this task.

Record the journal entries required within the general ledger to deal with the items below.

You should:

- **remove any incorrect entries, as appropriate**
- **post the correct entries**

Note: You do NOT need to give narratives.
Do NOT enter zeros into unused column cells.

> **Picklist for all journals below:** Commission expenses, Commission income, Bank, Accrued expenses, Prepaid expenses, Irrecoverable debts, Buildings at cost, Purchases ledger control account, Closing inventory (profit or loss), Closing inventory (financial position), Sales, Sales ledger control account, Suspense, Allowance for doubtful debts, Allowance for doubtful debts – adjustment, Balance b/d, Balance c/d.

(a) No entries have been made for closing inventory for the year ended 30 June 20X7. Closing inventory is valued at a cost of £5,320. Included in this amount is some inventory items that cost £750 that can only be sold for £600.

(6 marks)

Account	Dr £	Cr £
⬍		
⬍		

(b) A bank receipt for commission received of £7,920 has been correctly posted to the bank. No other entries were made.

(3 marks)

Account	Dr £	Cr £

(c) An irrecoverable debt for £1,342 needs to be written off for the year ended 30 June 20X7.

(3 marks)

Account	Dr £	Cr £

(d) A cheque received from a credit customer for £5,750 was dishonoured by the bank on the last day of the accounting period. No adjustment has been made in the cash book.

(3 marks)

Account	Dr £	Cr £

(e) A ledger balance of £800 for prepaid expenses was extracted incorrectly when included in the trial balance. The correct balance should be £1,000.

(3 marks)

Account	Dr £	Cr £

(f) The total column of the sales daybook of £36,922 was undercast by £200.

(3 marks)

Account	Dr £	Cr £

(g) Which ONE of the following is FALSE regarding the reasons for performing a bank reconciliation. Choose ONE answer only.

(2 marks)

a) Detecting errors such as missed payments and calculation errors
b) To help spot fraudulent transactions and theft
c) To keep an accurate record for accounts payable and receivables
d) Keeps the general ledger nice and clean without any details

---

End of Task

Task 5 (20 marks)

This task is about period end routines, using accounting records, and the extended trial balance.

You are preparing a purchases ledger control account reconciliation for a sole trader for the year ended 31 May 20X7.

The balance showing on purchases ledger control account is a credit of £37,998. The total supplier account balances in the purchase's ledger are a credit of £38,178.

The purchases ledger has been compared with purchases ledger control account and the following adjustments have been identified:

1.	Discounts received of £2,120 has been entered in the purchases ledger accounts of suppliers, but omitted as a posting to the purchase ledger control account.
2.	A BACS payment of £1,450 was debited to the purchase ledger account of ABC Ltd instead of the purchase ledger account of Axy Ltd.
3.	A BACS payment was made to a credit supplier for £900, but the amount that should have been paid was £920.
4.	A cheque for £3,000 sent to a supplier E. Edwards, was returned by the bank because it was unsigned. The correct entry for the returned cheque was made in the purchase ledger account of the supplier, but omitted from the purchase ledger control account.
5.	Purchase returns of £1,400 have been credited in error to the purchase ledger account of ZX Ltd, the correct entry was made in the purchase ledger control account.
6.	A set-off entry of £3,500 was omitted from purchases ledger control account, but was entered in the purchase ledger account of R. White correctly.

(a) Use the following table to show the THREE adjustments that should appear in the purchases ledger control account. Enter only ONE figure for each line. Do not enter zeros in unused cells.

(6 marks)

Account	Dr £	Cr £
⬇		
⬇		
⬇		

Picklist: Adjustment 1, Adjustment 2, Adjustment 3, Adjustment 4, Adjustment 5, Adjustment 6.

(b) Which ONE of the following statements about a wages control account is TRUE.

(3 marks)

The wages control account…

… is a general ledger account containing only summary amounts.	☐
… enables the matching of balances for a cash account to the corresponding information on a bank statement.	☐
… is used to monitor the amounts owed by customers to the business.	☐
…is an account where all detailed payroll transactions are posted for each employee.	☐

You are now working on the accounting records of a different business.

You have the following extended trial balance. The adjustments have already been correctly entered.

(c) Extend the figures into the columns for the statement of profit or loss and the statement of financial position. Do NOT enter zeros into unused column cells. Complete the extended trial balance by totalling the columns and entering any profit or loss figure for the year ended.

(11 marks)

Extended trial balance

Ledger account	Ledger balances		Adjustments		Statement of profit or loss		Statement of financial position	
	Dr £	Cr £	Dr £	Cr £	Dr £	Cr £	Dr £	Cr £
Bank	21932							
Opening inventory	6781							
Accrued income			600					
Capital		18527		6800				
Office expenses	4200							
Staff wages	16339							
Discounts allowed	477							
Discounts received		540		600				
Carriage outwards	1540							
Loan		30000		270				
Closing inventory			5000	5000				
Depreciation charges			3959					
Van at cost	17400		6800					
Van accumulated depreciation		6090		3959				
Purchases	45688							
Purchase ledger control account		5999	500					
Sales		79991						
Sales ledger control account	24090			500				
Loan interest paid	2700		270					
⊔								
Total	141147	141147	17129	17129	0	0	0	0

⊔ **Picklist**
Profit/loss for the year
Suspense
Balance b/d
Balance c/d
Gross profit/loss for the year

End of Task

Mock Exam Four - Solutions
AAT L3 Advanced Book-keeping

You may find the following tutor notes useful when answering exam practice tasks.

Elements of the financial statements

Five elements make up the general ledger accounts and financial statements of a business.

Assets

A resource controlled by the business as a result of past events and from which future economic benefits (money) are expected to flow to the business.

- Premises, machines, motor vehicles, office equipment or furniture and fittings.
- Inventory currently for resale.
- Trade receivables (money to be 'received') also called sales ledger control account.
- Accrued income.
- Prepaid expenses.
- Money in the bank.
- Cash in hand.

Liabilities

A present obligation of the business arising from past events, the settlement of which is expected to result in an outflow from the business.

- VAT owed to HMRC
- Wages owed to staff
- Bank loans and overdrafts
- Trade payables (money to be 'paid') also called purchases ledger control account.
- Prepaid income.
- Accrued expenses.

Capital

The residual interest (whatever is left) from the assets of the business after deducting all of its liabilities. Total assets less total liabilities is equal to capital (also called 'net assets') of the business. This balance represents what is owed and accumulated by the business to its owner. A separate account for drawings can also be maintained in the general ledger, drawings is money taken from the business by the owner and rather than reducing the owners capital account for the money taken, a drawings account is kept as a separate account because it provides more information.

Income

Money earned or received by the business from the sale of goods or services that is makes or sells (its trade), or from other investments or trade sources.

- Cash sales (sales not on credit).
- Credit sales (sales on credit).
- Rent received from ownership and rental of premises.
- Bank interest received.
- Discounts received (PPD) from paying credit suppliers early.
- Commission received.

Expenses

Costs incurred or paid for by the business in the normal course of trade in order to earn income. The cost of goods sold and other expenses must be matched with the sales revenues earned in the same period.

- Cash purchases (inventory purchases for resale and not on credit).
- Credit purchases (inventory purchases for resale and on credit).
- Rent payments (if the business is renting a property).
- Staff wages
- Motor vehicle running costs.
- Advertising.
- Depreciation such as wear and tear or loss of value to long-term assets such as machines or motor vehicles.
- Bank interest and charges.
- Discounts allowed (PPD) to credit customers who pay early.
- Accountancy and legal services.
- Irrecoverable debts expense.
- Increase (debit)/Decrease (credit) in allowances for doubtful debts.

Income and expenses are used to work out the amount of profit the business has generated. Any profits are owed to the owner of the business and increase the capital account of the owner.

DEAD CLIC

Don't get clouded in the double entry logic, ledgers are balances kept for the five elements of the financial statements and we are increasing or decreasing these balances according to the rules of double entry.

Important double entry terminology

DEAD CLIC defines what is the 'normal balance' or the natural state for a T account (general, sales or purchase ledger account).

DEAD CLIC is an acronym which gives the elements of financial statements and whether each element would be a debit or credit balance overall within a double entry ledger system. It can be used for determining the correct debit or credit balance but the element must be determined first. It can also be used to determine the correct double entry to increase or decrease an account balance.

DEAD CLIC

Debit	Credit
Expenses	Liabilities
Assets	Income
Drawings	Capital

The elements	Natural state	Increase balance (as per the natural state)	Decrease balance (opposite to natural state)
Income	Credit	Credit	Debit
Expenses	Debit	Debit	Credit
Assets	Debit	Debit	Credit
Liabilities	Credit	Credit	Debit
Capital	Credit	Credit	Debit

Totalling and balancing ledger accounts

1. Look at both sides of the ledger account and find the side which has the biggest total amount (debits or credits).
2. Add up the 'total' of all the entries on the side that has the biggest total amount and put this 'total' amount on both sides of the ledger account.
3. Add up all the entries on the side of the ledger account that had the smallest total amount.
4. Work out on the side that had the smallest total amount, the difference between the total amount entered and the other entries made on this side. This is the balance carried down (c/d) at the end of the period.
5. The balance c/d is entered on the side of the ledger account that had the smallest total amount to ensure that both total amounts entered on either side of the ledger account agrees. This as an arithmetical control and considered good practice in manual ledger accounting.

The balance c/d is only a balancing figure to ensure both sides of the ledger account agree at the end of the period. The true debit or credit balance is brought down (b/d) on the opposite side to the balance carried down (c/d). The balance b/d is on the 1st (beginning) of the month and the balance c/d is at the end of the month 30th/31st (ignoring February).

The trial balance and errors

The purpose of a trial balance is to ensure that all entries made in an organisation's general ledger are properly balanced and to check the accuracy of entries made before a final set of financial accounts are produced. If the totals for debit and credit balances do not agree then errors have definitely occurred, but even if the totals for debit and credit balances do agree it does not guarantee the general ledger balances are free from errors or omissions.

Types of errors not disclosed by the trial balance

The following types of error all have one thing in common, the same amount has been debited and credited within the general ledger, but an error has still occurred. These type of errors do not cause an imbalance when a trial balance is prepared (total debits equal total credits in the trial balance). Types of errors not disclosed by the trial balance can be remembered using the acronym 'TOPCROC'. Because the trial balance will still balance these types of error are more difficult to detect.

- **T Transposition** (two or more digits are reversed when amounts are entered).
- **O Original entry** (errors occur when documents such as invoices or credit notes are prepared incorrectly or when erroneous documents are posted to the day books).
- **P Principle** (mis posting to the WRONG ledger account and WRONG financial element), for example an 'expense' debited instead to an 'asset', a fundamental error because assets and profits will be under or overstated.
- **C Commission** (mis posting to the WRONG ledger account but RIGHT financial element), for example an 'expense' debited instead to another type of 'expense', less fundamental than an error of principle because assets and profits will be not be under or overstated.
- **R Reversal of entries** (the debit and credit mis posted the wrong way around).
- **O Omission** of a transaction (no posting made in the general ledger).
- **C Compensating** errors (very rare but this can happen), two independent errors for two different amounts posted as a debit and credit, the two errors compensate and cancel each other out. The trial balance will still balance.

Types of errors disclosed by the trial balance

The following types of error all have one thing in common, they all cause an imbalance when a trial balance is prepared (total debits do not equal total credits in the trial balance). Types of errors disclosed by the trial balance can be remembered using the acronym 'TESCOS'.

- **T Transposition** e.g. error posted incorrectly on one side of a ledger account but correctly posted on the other side such as debit expenses £54 and credit bank £45.
- **E Extraction** e.g. a ledger balance is not totalled and balanced correctly, so the wrong ledger balance is now 'extracted' and represented incorrectly in the trial balance.
- **S Single entry** e.g. a debit entry posted, but no credit entry posted, or vice versa.
- **C Casting** (casting means 'adding') e.g. a column in a day book casted (added up) incorrectly and the incorrect amount posted to the general ledger.
- **O Omission** of a ledger balance within the trial balance e.g. a ledger balance completely missed out and not included in the trial balance.
- **S Same sided** e.g. 2 debit entries only posted in error, or 2 credit entries only posted in error, rather than a debit and a credit entry made correctly.

Examples of how suspense accounts are opened

Example 1

Trial Balance (totals before suspense account opened)	154,896	155,279
Suspense account opened (debit balance)	383	
Trial balance totals agree until error(s) found	155,279	155,279

Example 1 the trial balance does not balance. The suspense account is always opened for the difference that exists between debits and credits and to ensure debits equal credits. The larger amount is credit £155,279 and the smaller amount is debit £154,896. A debit amount of £155,279 - £154,896 = £383 is missing. A suspense account is opened as £383 debit balance to ensure the trial balance agrees and until the error(s) has been found.

Example 2

Trial Balance (totals before suspense account opened)	121,780	99,800
Suspense account opened (credit balance)		21,980
Trial balance totals agree until error(s) found	121,780	121,780

Example 2 the trial balance does not balance. The larger amount is debit £121,780 and the smaller amount is credit £99,800. A credit amount of £121,780 - £99,800 = £21,980 is missing. A suspense account is opened as £21,980 credit balance to ensure the trial balance agrees and until the error(s) has been found.

Task 1 (21 marks)

Part (a) (18 marks)

Description /Serial number	Acquisition date	Cost £	Depreciation charges £	Carrying amount £	Funding method	Disposal proceeds £	Disposal date
Plant and equipment							
Forklift TKO	04/02/X7	15500.00			Hire Purchase		
Year ended 30/09/X7			2712.50	12787.50			
Year ended 30/09/X8			1598.44	0.00		3400.00	24/03/X8
Forklift INDUX	**07/10/X7**	**20889.00**			**Hire Purchase**		
Year ended 30/09/X8			5744.48	15144.53			
Computer equipment							
Warehouse PCs	01/10/X5	8400.00			Bank Loan		
Year ended 30/09/X6			3360.00	5040.00			
Year ended 30/09/X7			2016.00	3024.00			
Year ended 30/09/X8			1209.60	1814.40			
Industrial fixtures							
Warehouse shelving	06/08/X6	25000.00			Bank Loan		
Year ended 30/09/X6			208.33	24791.67			
Year ended 30/09/X7			2500.00	22291.67			
Year ended 30/09/X8			2500.00	19791.67			

Forklift TKO (sold)

- The forklift would be removed from the accounting records of the business by posting both the original cost and accumulated depreciation for this asset to a disposal account. The carrying value would always be zero because the asset has been removed from the books of the business.
- Depreciation is calculated on an annual basis and charged in equal instalments for each full month the asset is owned in the year. Depreciation charged should be 5 months, it was owned in the accounting period 01/10/X7 to 24/03/X8 before sale which was for 5 full months of ownership. 30% x carrying value at the beginning of the year £12,787.50 = £3,836.25 depreciation charged for a year. £3,836.25 for the year ÷ 12 months = £319.6875 per month x 5 months = £1,598.44. Since you are dividing by 12 months and multiplying by 5 months, the quickest calculation would be 30% x £12,787.50 x 5/12 = £1598.44.
- The disposal proceeds would be recorded in the non-current asset register excluding any VAT. The VAT on this transaction be posted to the VAT control account. The correct date of sale (disposal) is also required to be entered in the non-current asset register.

Forklift INDUX (purchased in the year)

To: ABC Warehouse	From: INDU Suppliers Invoice number: 001239	Date: 7 October 20X7
Item	**Details**	**£**
Forklift INDUX		**19,950.00**
Weatherproof cover	for Forklift INDUX	**550.00**
Recharging kits for INDUX forklift	@ £144.50 each	**289.00**
Delivery		100.00
Net total		20,889.00
VAT 20%		4,177.80
Total		25,066.80
Hire purchase arrangement 17.6% interest rate per annum.		

Capitalisation cost for Forklift INDUX

- Forklift INDUX £19,950.00 is capital expenditure.

- The weatherproof cover and recharging kits for the forklift are also capital expenditure. Even though the recharging kits for the forklift cost per item below the threshold of £500 (the accounting policy for capitalising expenditure), the Forklift INDUX 'in aggregate' (in total) costs more than £500, so the entire asset along with all items that relate to it would be capitalised.

Using the example of a dining room table and 6 chairs for the dining room table. If purchased as a 'dining room set' then the individual items in particular the chairs, may each cost below the materiality threshold, but would be aggregated with the cost of the table and all expenditure capitalised. This is similar to the forklift and its cover and its recharging kits, it is treated as all one asset together all costing together greater than £500.

- Delivery cost is always capitalised with the asset.

- VAT should be ignored as the business will reclaim all VAT on the purchase. The VAT on this transaction be posted to the VAT control account.

- The total cost ignoring VAT that should be capitalised (items highlighted in red bold in the invoice above) would be £20,889.00.

Depreciation for Forklift INDUX

- Depreciation is calculated on an annual basis and charged in equal instalments for each full month the asset is owned in the year.
- Depreciation charged should be 11 months, it was owned in the accounting period 07/10/X7 to 30/09/X8 which was for 11 full months of ownership. 30% x carrying value at the beginning of the year £20,889.00 = £6,266.7 depreciation charged for a year. £6,266.7 for the year ÷ 12 months = £522.225 per month x 11 months = £5,744.48. Since you are dividing by 12 months and multiplying by 11 months, the quickest calculation would be 30% x £20,889.00 x 11/12 = £5,744.48.
- The carrying value at the year-end is £20,889.00 - £5,744.48 = £15,144.53.

Warehouse PCs

- Computer equipment is depreciated at 40% per annum on a diminishing balance basis.
- The carrying value at the beginning of the year was £3,024.00 x 40% = £1,209.60 depreciation.
- The carrying value at the year-end would be carrying value at the beginning of the year £3,024.00 - £1,209.60 depreciation charged in the year = £1,814.40.

Warehouse shelving

- Industrial fixtures are depreciated £25,000 over ten years on a straight-line basis assuming no residual value. Depreciation charges would be (original cost £25,000 less zero residual value) ÷ 10 years = £2,500.00.
- The carrying value at the year-end would be carrying value at the beginning of the year £22,291.67 - £2,500.00 depreciation charged in the year = £19,791.67.

Part (b) (3 marks)

Answer A. Authorisation. Authorisation is the process of giving someone permission to do something and it is necessary that an appropriate person in the organisation gives authority or approval prior to capital purchases being made.

Task 2 (17 marks)

(a) (i) Make entries in the accounts below for:

- **The acquisition of the new computer equipment**
- **The depreciation charge on the new computer equipment**
- **The disposal of the old computer equipment**

(11 marks)

- The new computer equipment was purchased for £8,400 on 23 November 20X2.
- Computer equipment is depreciated at 30% per annum on a diminishing balance basis.
- A full year's depreciation is charged in the year of acquisition. £8,400 x 30% = depreciation £2,520.

Computers at cost

	£		£
Balance b/d	9200	Disposals	9200
Bank	8400	Balance c/d	8400
	17600		17600

Computers accumulated depreciation

	£		£
Disposals	4722	Balance b/d	4722
Balance c/d	2520	Depreciation charges	2520
	7242		7242

Depreciation charges

	£		£
Computers accumulated depreciation	2520	Profit or loss account	2520
	2520		2520

Disposals

	£		£
Computers at cost	9200	Computers accumulated depreciation	4722
		Bank	1500
		Profit or loss account	2978
	9200		9200

(a) (ii) Complete the following sentence.

A gain was earned from the disposal of the old computer equipment.
(Select: TRUE or FALSE)

The above statement is false because the old computer equipment was sold for less than its carrying value. The carrying value was £9,200 - £4,722 = £4,478. The sale proceeds were £1,500. The loss transferred to the profit or loss account for the year would be £4,478 - £1,500 = £2,978. In accounting terms there is a debit balance remaining in the disposals account of £2,978 to remove and transfer to the profit or loss account for the year ended. A debit balance indicates this is an expense (debit) not income (credit).

(b) For the year ended complete the following calculations relating to the processing plant for its first year of operation. Round each answer to one decimal place.

(5 marks)

(i) Calculate the depreciation charge for the plants first year of operation.

£0.4.

(ii) Calculate the carrying value at the end of the first year.

£11.6.

The units of production method for depreciation gives a depreciation charge based on the number of units produced over the assets useful life. It uses residual value in its working similar to the straight-line method.

£12m - £2m = £10m depreciable amount ÷ 50m barrels = £0.20m per barrel produced. £0.20 per barrel x 2 million barrels produced = depreciation £400,000 (£0.4 million).

Depreciation charge =
(£12m - £2m) x 2 / 50 = £0.4 million.

Carrying value =
£12 million cost - £0.4 million depreciation = £11.6 million.

Task 3 (19 marks)

(a) Update the interest income account.

Show clearly:

- **the cash book figure**
- **the year end adjustment**
- **the transfer to the statement of profit or loss for the year.**

(6 marks)

Interest income

	£		£
Accrued income (reversal)	80	Bank	360
Profit or loss account	320	Accrued income	40
	400		400

The cash book for the year shows receipts for interest income of £360, debit bank and credit interest income with £360 received.

- The £360 does not include £120 of interest earned for the period 01/03/X5 to 31/05/X5. 01/03/X5 to 31/03/X5 is one month's interest that has been earned but not received for the year ended 31 March 20X5.
- This is accrued income and we need to prorate the £120 earned for three months and calculate how much has been earned in one month.
- £120 ÷ 3 months = £40 earned per month.
- £40 x 1 month earned in the accounting year but not received = £40 accrued income.

Accrued income is money earned but not received by the business (an asset). The double entry to record the interest earned which is omitted in the books of the business for the year ended would be to debit accrued income (increase assets in the statement of financial position) and credit interest income (increasing income in the profit or loss account). Assets increase by £40 and income increases by £40.

(b) Answer the following regarding the accrued income (reversal) of £80 in (a) above.

(4 marks)

(i) How are the elements of the accounting equation effected by this transaction. Tick ONE box for each row.

Accrued income is money earned but not received. The double entry is to debit accrued income and credit interest income. An accrued income (reversal) is made as an accounting entry at the beginning of an accounting period and would be the opposite entry. The double entry is to debit interest income and credit accrued income. A reversal therefore causes assets (accrued income) to now decrease and income (interest income) to decrease. A decrease in income will cause a fall in profit and less capital owed to the owner of the business.

	Increase	Decrease	No change
Assets	☐	☑	☐
Liabilities	☐	☐	☑
Capital	☐	☑	☐

(ii) Which ONE of the following dates should be entered for this transaction in the ledger account shown in (a) above.

The 'reversal' of accruals and prepayments are always entries made in the ledger accounts on the first day of the accounting period. This business has a year end of 31 March 20X5 the beginning of this accounting period would be 1 April 20X4.

31 March 20X5	☐
1 April 20X5	☐
1 April 20X4	☑

(c) (i) Calculate electricity expenses for the year ended 31 March 20X5 and complete the table shown below. If necessary, use a minus sign to indicate ONLY the deduction of an amount from the cash book figure.

(3 marks)

To understand the logic of the calculations needed to complete this question, a good approach is to draw up a ledger account working. Bank payments of £3,042 are being adjusted for accrued expenses of £342 (expenses consumed but not paid for) to find the amount charged to the profit and loss account for the year ended 31 March 20X5. You can see from the account below that £342 is being added to £3,042 on the same side of the account and £498 is deducted (the reversal on the opposite side of the account) to find the amount charged to the profit or loss account as an expense for the year-ended.

Electricity expenses

	£		£
Bank	3042	Accrued expenses (reversal)	498
Accrued expenses	352	Profit or loss account	2896
	3394		3394

	£
Cash book figure	3042
Opening adjustment	-498
Closing adjustment	352
Electricity expenses for the year ended 31/03/X5	2896

(c) (ii) Drag and drop the account names to the debit and credit columns to show the entries for providing for accrued expenses of £352 for the year end 31 March 20X5.

(3 marks)

The above ledger account working shows the double entry for the accrual of £352. It is a debit entry to electricity expenses (increasing expenses in the profit or loss account) and a credit entry to accrued expenses (increasing a liability in the statement of financial position).

Debit
Electricity expenses

Credit
Accrued expenses

(d) Which ONE of the following is the least likely action that Jacob should take following this interview.

(3 marks)

Answer (a) She shows good business acumen and promise, offer her the job. Jacob should not offer her the job because she clearly lacks integrity as indicated by her willingness to breach confidentiality. Furthermore, because she would breach the fundamental principles of integrity and confidentiality, Jacob should report her to the AAT.

Task 4 (23 marks)

The first tip with journal entries is to make sure all rows are completed in the exam task for example, 4 journal rows indicate that 4 entries will need to be completed.

The second tip is for the correction of suspense account errors. There are three different ways we can adjust for a suspense account error, so the number of rows included in the journal for correction of the error should help to guide you.

Three different ways to correct a suspense account error

- Adjust the error as a single adjustment between the suspense account and the incorrect account (2 rows). For example, if the bank had been credited correctly with £1,000 but motor vehicle expenses had been debited incorrectly with £900. Then debit motor vehicle expenses £100 and credit the suspense account £100.

- Reverse the whole amount of the error and correct the error for the whole amount, then bring any difference between these two entries as a single entry to the suspense account (3 rows). For example, if the bank had been credited correctly with £1,000 but motor vehicle expenses had been debited incorrectly with £900. Reverse the error by 'crediting' motor vehicle expenses with £900, correct the error by 'debiting' motor expenses with £1,000. The £100 'credit' remaining is posted to the suspense account to complete the double entry.

- Reverse the whole amount of the error and post the entry to the opposite side of the suspense account to complete the double entry. Correct the error for the whole amount and post the entry to the opposite side of the suspense account to complete the double entry (4 rows). For example, if the bank had been credited correctly with £1,000 but motor vehicle expenses had been debited incorrectly with £900. Reverse the error by 'crediting' motor vehicle expenses with £900 and debiting the suspense account with £900. Correct the error by 'debiting' motor vehicle expenses with £1,000 and crediting the suspense account with £1,000.

(a) No entries have been made for closing inventory for the year ended 30 June 20X7. Closing inventory is valued at a cost of £5,320. Included in this amount is some inventory items that cost £750 that can only be sold for £600.

(6 marks)

Inventory is an asset (goods held for resale) and should always be valued at the lower of its purchase cost or net realisable value (NRV). NRV means what the inventory can be sold for and if this is lower than the original cost to the business then we value the inventory at NRV, not original cost. The accounting concept of prudence would value the inventory at £600 NRV in this case rather than its purchase cost of £750. This way we do not 'overstate' our asset values held in the statement of financial position, also the asset value has fallen so it would be prudent to devalue the inventory and to charge the fall in the value to the profit and loss account for the year. £5,320 - £750 + £600 = £5,170.

For the year end we need to represent an asset (goods unsold for the year), this is represented in the financial position (DR to increase assets). We also need a reduction for purchases expenses in the profit and loss account, for the unsold inventory (CR to decrease cost of sales as an expense).

Account	Dr £	Cr £
Closing inventory (financial position)	5170	
Closing inventory (profit or loss)		5170

(b) A bank receipt for commission received of £7,920 has been correctly posted to the bank. No other entries were made.

(3 marks)

Account	Dr £	Cr £
Commission income		7920
Suspense	7920	

To record income (commission received) you need to credit income. The bank has already recorded the money received, the debit entry to the bank £7,920 has already been posted. Due to no credit of £7,920 a suspense account would be opened to record the credit balance. It must now be reversed. We need to credit commission income and debit the suspense account to correct the entry.

The following workings may also help understand the logic.

Ledger account	HOW IT WAS Existing Balances		Journal		HOW IT SHOULD BE Revised Balances	
	Dr £	Cr £	Dr £	Cr £	Dr £	Cr £
Bank	7920				7920	
Commission income				7920		7920
Suspense		7920	7920			

(c) An irrecoverable debt for £1,342 needs to be written off for the year ended 30 June 20X7. (3 marks)

Account	Dr £	Cr £
Sales ledger control account		1342
Irrecoverable debts	1342	

The double entry for an irrecoverable debt is to debit irrecoverable debts (increasing expenses in the profit and loss account) and to credit the sales ledger control account (decreasing assets, which is the balance of money owed by customers). The debt also needs to be removed from the sales ledger account of the customer and the customer's account closed.

(d) A cheque received from a credit customer for £5,750 was dishonoured by the bank on the last day of the accounting period. No adjustment has been made in the cash book.

(3 marks)

A dishonoured cheque needs to be credited to the bank account (since the original cash receipt would have been recorded as a debit to the bank account) and debited to the sales ledger control account (SLCA) to increase this asset balance.

Account	Dr £	Cr £
Sales ledger control account	5750	
Bank		5750

(e) A ledger balance of £800 for prepaid expenses was extracted incorrectly when included in the trial balance. The correct balance should be £1,000.

(3 marks)

Prepaid expenses are expenses paid for and the benefit not consumed until a future accounting period. Prepaid expenses are an asset in the statement of financial position. It should be included as a debit (asset) of £1,000, but only a debit of £800 has been extracted. A suspense account would record the missing debit balance of £200 and this needs to be reversed.

Account	Dr £	Cr £
Prepaid expenses	200	
Suspense		200

The following workings may also help understand the logic.

Ledger account	The task information		The Solution required		To help work out the solution	
	HOW IT WAS		Journal		HOW IT SHOULD BE	
	Existing Balances				Revised Balances	
	Dr £	Cr £	Dr £	Cr £	Dr £	Cr £
Prepaid expenses	800		200		1000	
Suspense	200			200		

(f) The total column of the sales daybook of £36,922 was undercast by £200.

(3 marks)

The total column of the sales daybook is the value of all credit invoices issued to customers. The double entry to record these invoices is to debit the sales ledger control account (increasing the asset which is money owed by customers) and credit sales (increasing income) and credit VAT (increasing liability to pay HMRC). If the total column was undercast, this means it was under added by £200, so £200 in total was not posted as a debit to the sales ledger account. No mention of the other columns containing errors. Given that £200 was not posted as a debit entry then a suspense account would include a £200 debit balance to ensure the trial balance will balance.

Account	Dr £	Cr £
Sales ledger control account	200	
Suspense		200

The following workings may also help understand the logic.

	The task information		The Solution required		To help work out the solution	
	HOW IT WAS		Journal		HOW IT SHOULD BE	
Ledger account	Existing Balances				Revised Balances	
	Dr £	Cr £	Dr £	Cr £	Dr £	Cr £
Sales ledger control account	36992		200		37192	
Suspense	200			200		

(g) Which ONE of the following is FALSE regarding the reasons for performing a bank reconciliation. Choose ONE answer only.

(2 marks)

Answer (d) is false. Keeping the general ledger nice and clean without any details as its more likely to do with control account postings like the SLCA, PLCA or VAT control accounts. The totals from the books of prime entry are posted to control accounts to avoid unnecessary detail within the general ledger. All other reasons given are reasons for performing a bank reconciliation.

Task 5 (20 marks)

Part (a) 6 marks

This task can examine adjustments to a sales ledger control account (SLCA), purchase ledger control account (PLCA) or the cash book from reconciliations already undertaken in the task.

Account	Dr £	Cr £
Adjustment 1	2120	
Adjustment 4		3000
Adjustment 6	3500	

1.	Discounts received of £2,120 has been entered in the purchases ledger accounts of suppliers, but omitted as a posting to the purchase ledger control account. **DR PLCA £2,120 to decrease liabilities to suppliers.**
2.	A BACS payment of £1,450 was debited to the purchase ledger account of ABC Ltd instead of the purchase ledger account of Axy Ltd. **The wrong account but still a posting to both the PLCA and purchase ledgers, this adjustment will not affect any reconciliation between the PLCA and purchase ledger accounts for suppliers.**
3.	A BACS payment was made to a credit supplier for £900, but the amount that should have been paid was £920. **This is a payment error and both the PLCA and purchase ledgers have been updated by £900. So, this adjustment will not affect any reconciliation between the PLCA and purchase ledger accounts of suppliers. When a further payment is made then both ledgers will be adjusted in the future.**
4.	A cheque for £3,000 sent to a supplier E. Edwards, was returned by the bank because it was unsigned. The correct entry for the returned cheque was made in the purchase ledger account of the supplier, but omitted from the purchase ledger control account. **When a payment is made to a supplier the double entry is to reduce (credit) the bank (an asset) and reduce (debit) the PLCA (a liability), in this case the payment has been recorded but now is reversed.** **CR PLCA £3,000 to increase liability to suppliers.**
5.	Purchase returns of £1,400 have been credited in error to the purchase ledger account of ZX Ltd, the correct entry was made in the purchase ledger control account. **The correct entry was made in the PLCA. Purchase returns should be a debit not a credit in the purchase ledger accounts since they reduce liability to pay suppliers. The £1,400 has increased the purchase ledger account of the supplier but instead it should have decreased it by £1,400. So, 2 x £1,400 is needed to reduce the purchase ledger account, once to cancel the error and twice for the correct posting.**
6.	A set-off entry of £3,500 was omitted from purchases ledger control account, but was entered in the purchase ledger account of R. White correctly. **Set-off entries always reduce the PLCA (debit to reduce the liability) and reduce the SLCA (credit to reduce the asset). DR PLCA £3,500 to decrease liability to suppliers.**

A PLCA showing the adjustments and the reconciliation (agreement) to the total balances in the purchase ledger accounts has been shown below to aid logic and further understanding.

PLCA (Trade Payables)

	£		£
Adjustment 1	2120	Balance b/d	37998
Adjustment 6	3500	Adjustment 4	3000
Balance c/d	35378		
	40998		40998

Adjustments to purchase ledger accounts

	£
Total balances from purchase ledger accounts	38178
Adjustment 5	-2800
Revised (corrected) balance from PLCA	35378

Adjustments 2 and 3 are not reconciling items and therefore ignored in the process above.

Part (b) 3 marks

... is a general ledger account containing only summary amounts.	✓
... enables the matching of balances for a cash account to the corresponding information on a bank statement.	☐
... is used to monitor the amounts owed by customers to the business.	☐
...is an account where all detailed payroll transactions are posted for each employee.	☐

The wages control account is a general ledger account and records the summary amounts (totals) from the detailed payroll records of the business. The control account keeps the general ledger free of detail, but still has the correct balance for preparing the financial statements. It is used to also as a control to agree (reconcile) the amount of net salaries paid to staff. The second answer is more to do with a bank reconciliation. The third answer is more to do with a sales ledger control account. The fourth answer is more to do with a detailed payroll report for each employee.

Part (c) 11 marks

(c) Extend the figures into the columns for the statement of profit or loss and the statement of financial position. Do NOT enter zeros into unused column cells. Complete the extended trial balance by totalling the columns and entering any profit or loss figure for the year ended.

(11 marks)

Tutor note: the trial balance has two adjustments for closing inventory. The DR (an asset) for closing inventory to be included in the statement of financial position and a CR (reduction to purchases expenses) for closing inventory to be included within the statement of profit or loss for the year ended.

The exam will have autosum function for the trial balance totals, so you will not need to add up your columns in the exam task. There is also a picklist selection for the profit or loss for the year end which when the amount is included it should balance the last 4 columns of the ETB. If a profit for example below, then the profit amount is a debit to the statement of profit or loss (closing the profit or loss account for the year) and a credit (transfer) to the statement of financial position (increasing the capital account balance owed to the owner of the business).

Ledger account	Ledger balances		Adjustments		Statement of profit or loss		Statement of financial position	
	Dr £	Cr £	Dr £	Cr £	Dr £	Cr £	Dr £	Cr £
Bank	21932						21932	
Opening inventory	6781				6781			
Accrued income			600				600	
Capital		18527		6800				25327
Office expenses	4200				4200			
Staff wages	16339				16339			
Discounts allowed	477				477			
Discounts received		540		600		1140		
Carriage outwards	1540				1540			
Loan		30000		270				30270
Closing inventory			5000	5000		5000	5000	
Depreciation charges			3959		3959			
Van at cost	17400		6800				24200	
Van accumulated depreciation		6090		3959				10049
Purchases	45688				45688			
Purchase ledger control account		5999	500					5499
Sales		79991				79991		
Sales ledger control account	24090			500			23590	
Loan interest paid	2700		270		2970			
Profit/loss for the year ⊔					4177			4177
Total	141147	141147	17129	17129	86131	86131	75322	75322

Mock Exam Five
AAT L3 Advanced Book-keeping

Assessment information:

You have **2 hours** to complete this practice assessment.

This assessment contains **5 tasks** and you should attempt to complete **every** task.
Each task is independent. You will not need to refer to your answers to previous tasks.
Read every task carefully to make sure you understand what is required.

The standard rate of VAT is 20%.

Where the date is relevant, it is given in the task data.
Both minus signs and brackets can be used to indicate negative numbers **unless** task instructions say otherwise.

You must use a full stop to indicate a decimal point. For example, write 100.57 not 100,57 or 100 57
You may use a comma to indicate a number in the thousands, but you don't have to.
For example, 10000 and 10,000 are both acceptable.

Task 1 (21 marks)

This task is about non-current assets.

You are working on the accounting records of a business known as DOD Traders.

DOD Traders is a VAT registered business.

The business purchased new office equipment for an office room. The following is the relevant purchase invoice paid by cheque from the business bank account.

To: DOD Traders	From: XYZ Stationary Invoice number: DO34002	Date: 1 December 20X6
Item	**Details**	**£**
Printer XX56	XX56	650.00
Software	for printer XX56	29.00
Delivery and installation	for printer XX56	159.00
A4 paper		59.00
10 office chairs	£50 each	500.00
10 office desks	£180 each	1800.00
Net total		3197.00

VAT can be reclaimed on the purchase of all items shown in the purchase invoice above.

The following relates to PC ZX200 which is an old computer sold by the business during the accounting period.

Item description	PC ZX200
Date of purchase	01/09/X4
Date of sale	31/01/X7
Cash received	£200.00 plus VAT

DOD Traders has a policy of capitalising expenditure over £150.

- Computer equipment is depreciated over four years on a straight-line basis assuming a £300 residual value at the end of its useful life.
- Motor vehicles are depreciated at 20% per annum on a diminishing balance basis.
- Office equipment is depreciated at 15% per annum on a diminishing balance basis.
- A full year's depreciation is charged in the year of acquisition and none in the year of disposal.

(a) For the year ended 31 January 20X7, record the following in the extract from the non-current asset register of DOD Traders shown below.

- Any acquisitions of non-current assets
- Any disposals of non-current assets
- Depreciation

(18 marks)

Note: Not every cell will require an entry and not all cells will accept entries. Choose answers where a grey picklist is given and insert figures into highlighted grey cells.
Show your numerical answers to TWO decimal places.
Use DD/MM/YY format for any dates.

Description /Serial number	Acquisition date	Cost £	Depreciation charges £	Carrying amount £	Funding method	Disposal proceeds £	Disposal date
Computer equipment							
PC ZX100	01/09/X4	1300.00			Cash		
Year ended 31/01/X5			250.00	1050.00			
Year ended 31/01/X6			250.00	800.00			
Year ended 31/01/X7							
PC ZX200	01/09/X4	1800.00			Cash		
Year ended 31/01/X5			375.00	1425.00			
Year ended 31/01/X6			375.00	1050.00			
Year ended 31/01/X7							Picklist 1 ⬇
Office equipment							
Picklist 3 ⬇	Picklist 2 ⬇				Picklist 4 ⬇		
Year ended 31/01/X7							
Motor vehicles							
Car RBV007	23/01/X6	16700.00			Hire Purchase		
Year ended 31/01/X6			3340.00	13360.00			
Year ended 31/01/X7							

Picklist 1 ⬇	Picklist 2 ⬇	Picklist 3 ⬇	Picklist 4 ⬇
31/01/X7	01/12/X6	Furniture and printer	Cash
01/12/X6	31/01/X7	Furniture	Lease
01/09/X4	01/09/X4	Printer	Hire Purchase

(b) Complete the following multiple-choice question. (3 marks)

Tom is an AAT student who works in the finance department of DOD Traders and is attending his best friend's wedding. He had a conversation with another wedding guest who worked at a local car dealership. The guest asked Tom if he could tell him how much DOD Traders spends on new cars every year.

If Tom was to give this information to the wedding guest then what fundamental ethical principle would Tom more likely be in breach of. Choose ONE answer only.

    a) Confidentiality
    b) Professional behaviour
    c) Integrity
    d) Objectivity

End of Task

Task 2 (17 marks)

This task is about ledger accounting for non-current assets.

You are working on the accounting records of a business for the year ended 31 May 20X5.

VAT can be ignored.

New fixtures and fittings were acquired by the business on 23 July 20X4. The cost was £38,900 and the purchase funded by a business bank loan. The business plans to sell the fixtures and fittings after 4 years when the residual value is expected to be worth £5,000.

A full year's depreciation is charged in the year of acquisition and none in the year of disposal. The cost and depreciation has already been entered below in the accounting records for existing fixtures and fittings, but does not include entries for the new fixtures and fittings.

Make entries in the accounts below for the acquisition and depreciation charge for the new fixtures and fittings for the year ended 31 May 20X5. For each account show clearly the balance to be carried down or transferred to the statement of profit or loss, as appropriate.

(a) (i) Calculate depreciation charges of the new fixtures and fittings for the year ended 31 May 20X5

£ [   ]

Make entries in the accounts below for:

- **The acquisition of the new fixtures and fittings**
- **The depreciation charge for the new fixtures and fittings**

(10 marks)

Fixtures and fittings at cost

	£			£
Balance b/d	19200		⇅	
⇅			⇅	
⇅			⇅	
	19200			0

Fixtures and fittings accumulated depreciation

	£			£
⇅		Balance b/d		3500
⇅			⇅	
⇅			⇅	
	0			3500

Depreciation charges

	£			£
⇅			⇅	
⇅			⇅	
⇅			⇅	
	0			0

(a) (ii) The depreciation rate for the year for the new fixtures and fittings as fraction and percentage would be 1/4 or 25% respectively.
(Select: TRUE **or** FALSE) (1 mark)

A business sold a van during its accounting period and a gain was made on its disposal.

(b) Drag and drop the account names to the debit and credit columns to show where the entries for the gain on disposal would be made.

(2 marks)

| Disposals |

| Debit | | Credit |

| Van at cost |

| Profit or loss account |

(c) Complete the following multiple-choice question. Select ONE answer only

(2 marks)

Depreciation of a non-current asset is least likely to be caused by which one of the following reasons:

a) Wear and tear
b) Obsolescence
c) Falling market values of similar assets
d) Rising prices for replacing similar assets

A business part-exchanged an old car during its accounting period in order to partly fund the acquisition of two more new cars for the business.

(d) Drag and drop the account names to the debit and credit columns to show where the entries for the part-exchange transaction on disposal would be made.

(2 marks)

Disposals

Debit

Credit

Motor vehicles at cost

Profit or loss account

End of Task

Task 3 (19 marks)

This task is about ledger accounting, including accruals and prepayments.

You are working on the accounting records of a business for the year ended 30 November 20X8.

You can ignore VAT in this task.

Business policy: accounting for accruals and prepayments
An entry is made to the income or expense account and an opposite entry to the relevant asset or liability account. In the following period, asset or liability entries are reversed.

You are looking at interest paid for the year.

- The cash book for the year shows payments for interest expenses of £7,092.
- Payments do not include £908 of interest payments which relates to the period 01/11/X8 to 30/11/X8.

(a) Update the interest payments expense account.

Show clearly:

- **the cash book figure**
- **the year end adjustment**
- **the transfer to the statement of profit or loss for the year.** (6 marks)

Interest payments

	£			£
⬍		Accrued expenses (reversal)		829
⬍			⬍	
⬍			⬍	
	0			829

Picklist: Interest payments, Interest receipts, Bank, Accrued expenses, Accrued income, Accrued income (reversal), Accrued expenses (reversal), Prepaid income, Statement of financial position, Prepaid income (reversal), Prepaid expenses (reversal), Profit or loss account, Prepaid expenses, Purchases ledger control account, Sales, Sales ledger control account, Balance b/d, Balance c/d.

(b) Answer the following regarding the accrued interest expense (reversal) of £829 in (a) above.

(4 marks)

(i) How are the elements of the accounting equation effected by this transaction. Tick ONE box for each row.

	Increase	Decrease	No change
Assets	☐	☐	☐
Liabilities	☐	☐	☐
Capital	☐	☐	☐

(ii) Which ONE of the following dates should be entered for this transaction in the ledger accounts in (a) above.

1 December 20X7	☐
30 November 20X8	☐
1 December 20X8	☐

The business received in its cash book for the accounting period £27,042 of commission income. It also had earned but not received £3,520 of commission income for the year ended 30 November 20X8. The business had an accrued income (reversal) for commission income at the beginning of the accounting period of £4,980.

(c) (i) Calculate the commission income included in the profit or loss account for the year ended 30 November 20X8 and complete the table shown below. If necessary, use a minus sign to indicate ONLY the deduction of an amount from the cash book figure.

(3 marks)

	£
Cash book figure	
Opening adjustment	
Closing adjustment	
Commission income received for the year ended 30/11/X8	

(c) (ii) Drag and drop the account names to the debit and credit columns to show where the ledger entries will be made for £3,520 of accrued income for the year ended 30 November 20X8.

(2 marks)

Accrued expenses

Commission income

Accrued income

Debit

Credit

(d) Enter the figures in the table shown below to the appropriate trial balance debit or credit columns.

Do not enter zeros in unused column cells. Do NOT use minus signs or brackets.

(4 marks)

Extract from the trial balance

Account	Ledger balance £	Trial balance £ DR	£CR
Prepaid income	1100		
Accrued expenses	902		
Prepaid expenses	1029		
Accrued income	1504		

End of Task

Task 4 (23 marks)

This task is about accounting adjustments.

You are a trainee accountant technician reporting to your manager in a finance department.

A trial balance has been drawn up and balanced using a suspense account. You now need to make some corrections and adjustments for the year ended 31 March 20X5.

You may ignore VAT in this task.

(a) Record the following adjustments in the extract from the extended trial balance shown below.

(16 marks)

- Irrecoverable debts of £3,420 are to be written off for the year ended 31 March 20X5.
- A rent payment of £1,000 has been incorrectly debited to the cashbook and credited to rent expenses.
- The purchase ledger control account was correctly credited with £990 but the debit posting made to purchases, incorrectly entered as £1,071.
- Accumulated depreciation has been correctly recorded as £1,511 for the year ended 31 March 20X5. No posting has been made to depreciation charges.
- Motor expenses of £80 should be posted to drawings.

Extract from the extended trial balance

Ledger account	Ledger balances		Adjustments	
	Dr £	Cr £	Dr £	Cr £
Bank		5699		
Opening inventory	4790			
Irrecoverable debts				
Capital		34922		
Motor expenses	4200			
Payroll costs	16339			
Rent expenses	10000			
Drawings	21339			
Depreciation charges				
Office equipment at cost	17400			
Office equipment accumulated depreciation		6090		
Purchases	12688			
Purchase ledger control account		6627		
Sales		66278		
Sales ledger control account	15900			
Suspense	1430			

An allowance for doubtful debts needs to be adjusted to 1.5% of outstanding trade receivables for the year ended 31 March 20X5.

(b) Calculate the value of the adjustment required (to the nearest £). Show the journal entries that will be required for the year ended 31 March 20X5 and select an appropriate narrative.

(4 marks)

Journal

Account	Dr £	Cr £
⬍		
⬍		

Picklist for journal: Allowance for doubtful debts, Allowance for doubtful debts - adjustment, Irrecoverable debts, Bank, Statement of financial position, Profit or loss account, Purchases ledger control account, Purchases, Sales, Sales ledger control account, Balance b/d, Balance c/d.

Narrative for journal

Picklist for narrative: Transfer to the profit or loss account, Provision for doubtful debts for the year ended 31 March 20X5, Closure of sales ledger control account for the year ended 31 March 20X5, Transfer to the suspense account.

Goods held for resale by the business were taken by the owner for her own personal use. No postings have been made.

(c) Drag and drop the account names to the debit and credit columns to show where the entries for the journal would be made.

(3 marks)

Drawings		Debit		Credit
Capital				
Purchases				

End of Task

Task 5 (20 marks)

This task is about period end routines, using accounting records, and the extended trial balance.

You are preparing a bank reconciliation for a business.

The balance showing on the bank statement is a debit of £3,285. The balance in the cash book is a credit of £7,033.

The bank statement has been compared with the cash book for the year ended 31 December 20X3 and the following points noted.

1.	A BACS payment to a supplier for the month of December 20X3 for £600 had not yet cleared the bank statements.
2.	Interest paid of £246 showing in the bank statements for the month of December 20X3 were not been entered in the cash book.
3.	A remittance advice from a customer has been received and an entry made in the cash book for the correct amount of £1,040. This is not yet showing on the bank statements.
4.	The bank has made an error. Interest paid of £246 for the month of December 20X3 has been in error debited twice on the bank statements.
5.	A faster payment of £3,460 has been recorded in the cash book in error as £3,640.
6.	A BACS receipt from a customer for £4,500 appears on the bank statements but was not recorded in the cash book.

(a) Use the following table to show the THREE adjustments that should be made as entries in the cash book. Enter only ONE figure for each line. Do not enter zeros in unused cells.

(6 marks)

Account	Dr £	Cr £
⬇		
⬇		
⬇		

Picklist: Item 1, Item 2, Item 3, Item 4, Item 5, Item 6.

(b) Drag and drop the account names to the debit and credit columns to show where the entries for total payroll costs for an accounting period should be made.

(3 marks)

| Wages expenses |
| Wages control |
| Bank |

Debit	Credit

You are now working on the accounting records of a different business.

You have the following extended trial balance. The adjustments have already been correctly entered.

(c) Extend the figures into the columns for the statement of profit or loss and the statement of financial position. Do NOT enter zeros into unused column cells. Complete the extended trial balance by totalling the columns and entering any profit or loss figure for the year ended.

(11 marks)

Extended trial balance

Ledger account	Ledger balances		Adjustments		Statement of profit or loss		Statement of financial position	
	Dr £	Cr £	Dr £	Cr £	Dr £	Cr £	Dr £	Cr £
Bank overdraft		8099		1400				
Fixtures and fittings at cost	40000							
Fixtures and fittings accumulated depreciation		8000		4000				
Purchases	44322							
Purchase ledger control account		4398		88				
Sales		87000						
Sales ledger control account	5000							
Rent expenses	10000		2000					
Staff wages	5040			2000				
Light and heat	2391							
Depreciation charges			4000					
VAT		4724	1545					
Miscellaneous expenses	449							
Opening inventory	1300							
Accruals				2000				
Capital		14338						
Closing inventory			2322	2322				
Drawings	18000		2000					
Suspense	57		1488	1545				
⬇								
Total	126559	126559	13355	13355	0	0	0	0

⬇ **Picklist**
Profit/loss for the year
Suspense
Balance b/d
Balance c/d
Gross profit/loss for the year

End of Task

5

Mock Exam Five
- Solutions
AAT L3 Advanced Book-keeping

You may find the following tutor notes useful when answering exam practice tasks.

Elements of the financial statements

Five elements make up the general ledger accounts and financial statements of a business.

Assets

A resource controlled by the business as a result of past events and from which future economic benefits (money) are expected to flow to the business.

- Premises, machines, motor vehicles, office equipment or furniture and fittings.
- Inventory currently for resale.
- Trade receivables (money to be 'received') also called sales ledger control account.
- Accrued income.
- Prepaid expenses.
- Money in the bank.
- Cash in hand.

Liabilities

A present obligation of the business arising from past events, the settlement of which is expected to result in an outflow from the business.

- VAT owed to HMRC
- Wages owed to staff
- Bank loans and overdrafts
- Trade payables (money to be 'paid') also called purchases ledger control account.
- Prepaid income.
- Accrued expenses.

Capital

The residual interest (whatever is left) from the assets of the business after deducting all of its liabilities. Total assets less total liabilities is equal to capital (also called 'net assets') of the business. This balance represents what is owed and accumulated by the business to its owner. A separate account for drawings can also be maintained in the general ledger, drawings is money taken from the business by the owner and rather than reducing the owners capital account for the money taken, a drawings account is kept as a separate account because it provides more information.

Income

Money earned or received by the business from the sale of goods or services that is makes or sells (its trade), or from other investments or trade sources.

- Cash sales (sales not on credit).
- Credit sales (sales on credit).
- Rent received from ownership and rental of premises.
- Bank interest received.
- Discounts received (PPD) from paying credit suppliers early.
- Commission received.

Expenses

Costs incurred or paid for by the business in the normal course of trade in order to earn income. The cost of goods sold and other expenses must be matched with the sales revenues earned in the same period.

- Cash purchases (inventory purchases for resale and not on credit).
- Credit purchases (inventory purchases for resale and on credit).
- Rent payments (if the business is renting a property).
- Staff wages
- Motor vehicle running costs.
- Advertising.
- Depreciation such as wear and tear or loss of value to long-term assets such as machines or motor vehicles.
- Bank interest and charges.
- Discounts allowed (PPD) to credit customers who pay early.
- Accountancy and legal services.
- Irrecoverable debts expense.
- Increase (debit)/Decrease (credit) in allowances for doubtful debts.

Income and expenses are used to work out the amount of profit the business has generated. Any profits are owed to the owner of the business and increase the capital account of the owner.

DEAD CLIC

Don't get clouded in the double entry logic, ledgers are balances kept for the five elements of the financial statements and we are increasing or decreasing these balances according to the rules of double entry.

Important double entry terminology

DEAD CLIC defines what is the 'normal balance' or the natural state for a T account (general, sales or purchase ledger account).

DEAD CLIC is an acronym which gives the elements of financial statements and whether each element would be a debit or credit balance overall within a double entry ledger system. It can be used for determining the correct debit or credit balance but the element must be determined first. It can also be used to determine the correct double entry to increase or decrease an account balance.

DEAD CLIC

Debit	Credit
Expenses	Liabilities
Assets	Income
Drawings	Capital

The elements	Natural state	Increase balance (as per the natural state)	Decrease balance (opposite to natural state)
Income	Credit	Credit	Debit
Expenses	Debit	Debit	Credit
Assets	Debit	Debit	Credit
Liabilities	Credit	Credit	Debit
Capital	Credit	Credit	Debit

Totalling and balancing ledger accounts

1. Look at both sides of the ledger account and find the side which has the biggest total amount (debits or credits).
2. Add up the 'total' of all the entries on the side that has the biggest total amount and put this 'total' amount on both sides of the ledger account.
3. Add up all the entries on the side of the ledger account that had the smallest total amount.
4. Work out on the side that had the smallest total amount, the difference between the total amount entered and the other entries made on this side. This is the balance carried down (c/d) at the end of the period.
5. The balance c/d is entered on the side of the ledger account that had the smallest total amount to ensure that both total amounts entered on either side of the ledger account agrees. This as an arithmetical control and considered good practice in manual ledger accounting.

The balance c/d is only a balancing figure to ensure both sides of the ledger account agree at the end of the period. The true debit or credit balance is brought down (b/d) on the opposite side to the balance carried down (c/d). The balance b/d is on the 1st (beginning) of the month and the balance c/d is at the end of the month 30th/31st (ignoring February).

The trial balance and errors

The purpose of a trial balance is to ensure that all entries made in an organisation's general ledger are properly balanced and to check the accuracy of entries made before a final set of financial accounts are produced. If the totals for debit and credit balances do not agree then errors have definitely occurred, but even if the totals for debit and credit balances do agree it does not guarantee the general ledger balances are free from errors or omissions.

Types of errors not disclosed by the trial balance

The following types of error all have one thing in common, the same amount has been debited and credited within the general ledger, but an error has still occurred. These type of errors do not cause an imbalance when a trial balance is prepared (total debits equal total credits in the trial balance). Types of errors not disclosed by the trial balance can be remembered using the acronym 'TOPCROC'. Because the trial balance will still balance these types of error are more difficult to detect.

- **T Transposition** (two or more digits are reversed when amounts are entered).
- **O Original entry** (errors occur when documents such as invoices or credit notes are prepared incorrectly or when erroneous documents are posted to the day books).
- **P Principle** (mis posting to the WRONG ledger account and WRONG financial element), for example an 'expense' debited instead to an 'asset', a fundamental error because assets and profits will be under or overstated.
- **C Commission** (mis posting to the WRONG ledger account but RIGHT financial element), for example an 'expense' debited instead to another type of 'expense', less fundamental than an error of principle because assets and profits will be not be under or overstated.
- **R Reversal of entries** (the debit and credit mis posted the wrong way around).
- **O Omission** of a transaction (no posting made in the general ledger).
- **C Compensating** errors (very rare but this can happen), two independent errors for two different amounts posted as a debit and credit, the two errors compensate and cancel each other out. The trial balance will still balance.

Types of errors disclosed by the trial balance

The following types of error all have one thing in common, they all cause an imbalance when a trial balance is prepared (total debits do not equal total credits in the trial balance). Types of errors disclosed by the trial balance can be remembered using the acronym 'TESCOS'.

- **T Transposition** e.g. error posted incorrectly on one side of a ledger account but correctly posted on the other side such as debit expenses £54 and credit bank £45.
- **E Extraction** e.g. a ledger balance is not totalled and balanced correctly, so the wrong ledger balance is now 'extracted' and represented incorrectly in the trial balance.
- **S Single entry** e.g. a debit entry posted, but no credit entry posted, or vice versa.
- **C Casting** (casting means 'adding') e.g. a column in a day book casted (added up) incorrectly and the incorrect amount posted to the general ledger.
- **O Omission** of a ledger balance within the trial balance e.g. a ledger balance completely missed out and not included in the trial balance.
- **S Same sided** e.g. 2 debit entries only posted in error, or 2 credit entries only posted in error, rather than a debit and a credit entry made correctly.

Examples of how suspense accounts are opened

Example 1

Trial Balance (totals before suspense account opened)	154,896	155,279
Suspense account opened (debit balance)	383	
Trial balance totals agree until error(s) found	155,279	155,279

Example 1 the trial balance does not balance. The suspense account is always opened for the difference that exists between debits and credits and to ensure debits equal credits. The larger amount is credit £155,279 and the smaller amount is debit £154,896. A debit amount of £155,279 - £154,896 = £383 is missing. A suspense account is opened as £383 debit balance to ensure the trial balance agrees and until the error(s) has been found.

Example 2

Trial Balance (totals before suspense account opened)	121,780	99,800
Suspense account opened (credit balance)		21,980
Trial balance totals agree until error(s) found	121,780	121,780

Example 2 the trial balance does not balance. The larger amount is debit £121,780 and the smaller amount is credit £99,800. A credit amount of £121,780 - £99,800 = £21,980 is missing. A suspense account is opened as £21,980 credit balance to ensure the trial balance agrees and until the error(s) has been found.

Task 1 (21 marks)

Part (a) (18 marks)

Description /Serial number	Acquisition date	Cost £	Depreciation charges £	Carrying amount £	Funding method	Disposal proceeds £	Disposal date
Computer equipment							
PC ZX100	01/09/X4	1300.00			Cash		
Year ended 31/01/X5			250.00	1050.00			
Year ended 31/01/X6			250.00	800.00			
Year ended 31/01/X7			250.00	550.00			
PC ZX200	01/09/X4	1800.00			Cash		
Year ended 31/01/X5			375.00	1425.00			
Year ended 31/01/X6			375.00	1050.00			
Year ended 31/01/X7			0.00	0.00		200.00	31/01/X7
Office equipment							
Furniture and printer	**01/12/X6**	**2638.00**			**Cash**		
Year ended 31/01/X7			395.70	2242.30			
Motor vehicles							
Car RBV007	23/01/X6	16700.00			Hire Purchase		
Year ended 31/01/X6			3340.00	13360.00			
Year ended 31/01/X7			2672.00	10688.00			

New furniture and printer

The amount that would be capitalised and included as non-current assets is bolded in red below:

Item	Details	£
Printer XX56	XX56	**650.00**
Software	for printer XX56	**29.00**
Delivery and installation	for printer XX56	**159.00**
A4 paper		59.00
10 office chairs	£50 each	500.00
10 office desks	£180 each	**1800.00**

Notes:

- Printer XX56 £650 is capital expenditure as it is expected to be used in the business beyond 12 months and is above the threshold of £150.

- The software is also capital expenditure. Even the though the software is below the threshold of £150, printer XX56 in aggregate costs (£650 + £29 + £159 = £838) more than £500, so the entire asset along with all items that relate to it would be capitalised.

Using the example of a dining room table and 6 chairs for the dining room table. If purchased as a 'dining room set' then the individual items in particular the chairs, may each cost below the materiality threshold, but would be aggregated with the cost of the table and all expenditure capitalised. This is similar to the printer, its software and delivery cost, it is treated as all one asset together all costing together greater than £150.

- Delivery and installation costs for non-current assets are capitalised with the cost of the printer. They should always be treated as capital expenditure.

- The printer paper is revenue not capital expenditure. Paper will be consumed by the business within 12 months and is treated as an expense rather than a non-current asset.

- The 10 office chairs are nothing to do with the printer as an aggregated asset and should not be capitalised because they each cost £50 each, which is below the £150 threshold for capitalising expenditure.

- The 10 office desks are nothing to do with the printer as an aggregated asset and should be capitalised because they each £180 which is above the £150 threshold for capitalising expenditure.

- The total amount of capitalised expenditure is therefore £2,638 (£650 + £29 + £159 + £1,800 = £2,638).

- The accounting policy is to apply a full years depreciation in the accounting year of purchase £2,638 x 15% depreciation rate = £395.70. The carrying value remaining at the end of the year would be £2,638 - £395.70 = £2,242.30.

PC ZX200 (sold)

- The computer would be removed from the accounting records of the business by posting both the cost and its accumulated depreciation of this asset to a disposal account. The carrying value would always be zero in the non-current asset register because the asset has been removed from the books of the business.

- No depreciation on this asset for the year-ended due to the policy of the business of none (0.00) charged in the year of disposal.

- The correct date of sale (disposal) and the disposal proceeds amount from sale are also required to be entered in the non-current asset register. Disposal proceeds would be recorded in the non-current asset register excluding any VAT, the VAT amount charged on this transaction would be posted to the VAT control account.

PC ZX100

- Computer PC ZX100 is depreciated over four years on a straight-line basis assuming a £300 residual value at the end of its useful life. Depreciation would be every year (£1,300 original cost - £300 residual value) = £1,000 ÷ 4 years = £250 depreciation charge per year.
- The carrying value at the beginning of the year £800 less depreciation for the year £250 = carrying value at the end of the year £550.

Motor vehicles

- Motor vehicles are depreciated at 20% per annum on a diminishing balance basis.
- The carrying value at the beginning of the year was £13,360.00 x 20% rate = £2,672.00 depreciation charges.
- The carrying value at the beginning of the year £13,360.00 less depreciation for the year £2,672.00 = carrying value at the end of the year £10,688.00.

Part (b) (3 marks)

Answer a). Confidentiality.
AAT members should respect the confidentiality of information acquired as a result of professional and business relationships and should not disclose any such information to third parties without proper and specific authority, unless there is a legal or professional right or duty to disclose. Confidential information acquired as a result of professional and business relationships should not be used for the personal advantage of members or third parties.

Task 2 (17 marks)

(a) (i) Calculate depreciation charges of the new fixtures and fittings for the year ended 31 May 20X5

£ | 8475

A full year's depreciation is charged in the year of acquisition. The new fixtures and fittings were acquired on 23 July 20X4.

The cost £38,900 - residual value (£5,000) = depreciable amount £33,900 ÷ 4 years useful life = depreciation charge for the year £8,475.

Make entries in the accounts below for:

- **The acquisition of the new fixtures and fittings**
- **The depreciation charge for the new fixtures and fittings**

(10 marks)

Fixtures and fittings at cost

	£		£
Balance b/d	19200	Balance c/d	58100
Bank loan	38900		
	58100		58100

Fixtures and fittings accumulated depreciation

	£		£
Balance c/d	11975	Balance b/d	3500
		Depreciation charges	8475
	11975		11975

Depreciation charges

	£		£
Fixtures and fittings accumulated depreciation	8475	Profit or loss account	8475
	8475		8475

(a) (ii) The depreciation rate for the year for the new fixtures and fittings as fraction and percentage would be 1/4 or 25% respectively.
(Select: TRUE)

(1 mark)

This would be true. 1 year of straight-line depreciation for every 4 years as a constant fraction each year is one quarter (1/4) and to convert a fraction to a percentage would be 1 ÷ 4 x 100% = 25% as a percentage rate of depreciation.

(b) Drag and drop the account names to the debit and credit columns to show where the entries for the gain on disposal would be made.

(2 marks)

Debit
Disposals

Credit
Profit or loss account

A gain on disposal would be income and a credit to the profit or loss account for income recognised. The opposite entry would be a debit to the disposals account where the gain (credit) is removed to close this account at the end of the accounting year.

(c) Complete the following multiple-choice question. Select ONE answer only

(2 marks)

Answer (d). Depreciate means to fall in value and the least likely reason would be rising prices for replacing similar assets. This would make a non-current asset more valuable not less valuable. The other three reasons would explain why a non-current asset would fall in value.

(d) Drag and drop the account names to the debit and credit columns to show where the entries for the part-exchange transaction on disposal would be made.

(2 marks)

A part-exchange means you pay less for a new asset by exchanging another asset. Because no cash is exchanged for a part exchange value, the amount needs to written into the accounting records of the business. Non-current assets (at cost) need to be debited to be increased by the part-exchange value given. The disposals account would be credited with the part-exchange value, just like if money had been received for its sale to calculate any gain or loss on disposal of the asset.

Debit
Motor vehicles at cost

Credit
Disposals

Task 3 (19 marks)

(a) Update the interest payments expense account.

Show clearly:

- **the cash book figure**
- **the year end adjustment**
- **the transfer to the statement of profit or loss for the year.**   (6 marks)

- The cash book for the year shows payments for interest expenses of £7,092. The entries would be debit expenses £7,092 and credit bank £7,092
- Payments do not include £908 of interest payments which relates to the period 01/11/X8 to 30/11/X8. The £908 is an expense consumed, but not paid for by the business during the year ended 30 November 20X8. The £908 is accrued expenses which is a liability of the business because the interest expense is owed by the business. There is no need to prorate the £908 as it fully relates to one month which is included in the accounting period. The entries would be debit expenses for the interest not recorded (increasing expenses for the year) and credit accrued expenses which is a liability represented in the statement of financial position, interest owed by the business.

Interest payments

	£		£
Bank	7092	Accrued expenses (reversal)	829
Accrued expenses	908	Profit or loss account	7171
	8000		8000

(b) Answer the following regarding the accrued interest expense (reversal) of £829 in (a) above.

(4 marks)

(i) How are the elements of the accounting equation effected by this transaction. Tick ONE box for each row.

	Increase	Decrease	No change
Assets			✓
Liabilities		✓	
Capital	✓		

For accrued expenses at the end of the year the double entry is debit expenses (increasing expenses) and credit accrued expenses (increasing liabilities). An accrued expenses (reversal) is an entry made on the first day of the accounting period and is the opposite to the entry made on the last day of the accounting period.

The accrued expense (reversal) of £829 is therefore on the credit side of the interest payments account (see the ledger account above) therefore reducing expenses charged to the profit or loss account for the accounting period. If expenses go down, then profits will go up and given profits increase the capital account, it will go up. The debit side would be posted to accrued expenses as a reversal (a liability in the statement of financial position) and this reduces liabilities for the period.

(ii) Which ONE of the following dates should be entered for this transaction in the ledger accounts in (a) above.

The 'reversal' of accruals and prepayments are always entries made in the ledger accounts on the first day of the accounting period. This business has a year end of 30 November 20X8 the beginning of this accounting period would be 1 December 20X7.

1 December 20X7	✓
30 November 20X8	☐
1 December 20X8	☐

(c) (i) Calculate the commission income included in the profit or loss account for the year ended 30 November 20X8 and complete the table shown below. If necessary, use a minus sign to indicate ONLY the deduction of an amount from the cash book figure.

(3 marks)

To understand the logic of the calculations needed to complete this question, a good approach is to draw up a ledger account working. Bank receipts of £27,042 are being adjusted for accrued income of £3,520 (income earned in the accounting period but not received) to find the amount included as income in the profit and loss account for the year ended 30 November 20X8. Accrued income is an asset because the business is owed £3,520 for commission income earned but not received, so debit accrued income and credit commission income which would increase income for the year.

You can see from the account below that the commission income (reversal) at the beginning of the accounting period of £4,980 is the opposite side of the account as we reverse the entry made from the pervious year, this reduces the amount included as income in the profit or loss account.

Commission income

	£		£
Accrued income (reversal)	4980	Bank	27042
Profit or loss account	25582	Accrued income	3520
	30562		30562

	£
Cash book figure	27042
Opening adjustment	-4980
Closing adjustment	3520
Commission income received for the year ended 30/11/X8	25582

(c) (ii) Drag and drop the account names to the debit and credit columns to show where the ledger entries will be made for £3,520 of accrued income for the year ended 30 November 20X8.

The above ledger account working shows the double entry for the accrued income of £3,520. A credit entry to commission income (in the profit or loss account) and a debit entry to accrued income (an asset in the statement of financial position).

(3 marks)

Debit
Accrued income

Credit
Commission income

(d) Enter the figures in the table shown below to the appropriate trial balance debit or credit columns.

Do not enter zeros in unused column cells. Do NOT use minus signs or brackets.

Extract from the trial balance

Account	Ledger balance £	Trial balance £ DR	£CR
Prepaid income (liability)	1100		1100
Accrued expenses (liability)	902		902
Prepaid expenses (asset)	1029	1029	
Accrued income (asset)	1504	1504	

Task 4 (23 marks)

(a) Record the following adjustments in the extract from the extended trial balance shown below.

(16 marks)

- Irrecoverable debts of £3,420 are to be written off for the year ended 31 March 20X5. **Double entry to record irrecoverable debts is to DR Irrecoverable debts (an expense in the statement of profit or loss) and CR SLCA (an asset in the statement of financial position).** The debt would also be removed from the sales ledger account balance of the customer and their account closed.

- A rent payment of £1,000 has been incorrectly debited to the cashbook and credited to rent expenses. **Correct double entry should have been DR Rent (increase expenses) and CR Bank (reduce asset). The entry has been recorded in reverse, so we need to DR Rent £1,000 and CR Bank £1,000 to reverse the incorrect entry and then DR Rent £1,000 and CR Bank £1,000 a second time to record the correct entry. Total entries required 2 x £1,000, DR Rent £2,000 and CR Bank £2,000.**

- The purchase ledger control account was correctly credited with £990 but the debit posting made to purchases, incorrectly entered as £1,071. **The debit posting to purchases should have been a debit of £990, so £1,071 - £990 = £81 debited too much. A suspense balance of £81 credit would be opened to balance the trial balance. We need to CR purchases £81 to correct and reduce the account and DR the suspense account £81 to remove the credit balance.**

- Accumulated depreciation has been correctly recorded as £1,511 for the year ended 31 March 20X5. No posting has been made to depreciation charges. **Double entry should have been DR Depreciation charges (expense in the statement of profit or loss) and CR Accumulated depreciation (an offset against the cost of non-current assets in the statement of financial position). The CR was entered but the DR of £1,511 to depreciation charges was not entered, so a suspense account balance of DR £1,511 would have been opened to ensure the trial balance would balance. DR £1,511 depreciation charges and CR £1,511 suspense account to remove the debit balance.**

- Motor expenses of £80 should be posted to drawings. **DR Drawings £80 and CR Motor expenses £80.**

Extract from the extended trial balance

Ledger account	Ledger balances		Adjustments	
	Dr £	Cr £	Dr £	Cr £
Bank		5699		2000
Opening inventory	4790			
Irrecoverable debts			3420	
Capital		34922		
Motor expenses	4200			80
Payroll costs	16339			
Rent expenses	10000		2000	
Drawings	21339		80	
Depreciation charges			1511	
Office equipment at cost	17400			
Office equipment accumulated depreciation		6090		
Purchases	12688			81
Purchase ledger control account		6627		
Sales		66278		
Sales ledger control account	15900			3420
Suspense	1430		81	1511

(b) Calculate the value of the adjustment required (to the nearest £). Show the journal entries that will be required for the year ended 31 March 20X5 and select an appropriate narrative.

(4 marks)

An allowance for doubtful debts needs to be adjusted to 1.5% of outstanding trade receivables for the year ended 31 March 20X5.

The allowance for doubtful debts is an account held in the financial position (always a credit balance) which is offset against the sales ledger control account (asset) also shown in the financial position (always a debit balance), the two balances are offset to find the net amount owed by credit customers.

The allowance for doubtful debts is calculated by applying a percentage of expected doubtful debts against the SLCA (asset) balance after accounting for any irrecoverable debts. In this task irrecoverable debts are provided for, so the balance of the SLCA is £15,900 after irrecoverable debts of £3,420 which would be a balance of £12,480.

The allowance for doubtful debts for the year end must be 1.5% of the SLCA balance (£12,480 x 1.5%) = £187 (to the nearest £1). **DR £187 allowance for doubtful debts – adjustment (increase expenses) and CR £187 allowance for doubtful debts (offset against the SLCA debit balance in the statement of financial position).**

Account	Dr £	Cr £
Allowance for doubtful debts		187
Allowance for doubtful debts - adjustment	187	

Narrative for journal

Provision for doubtful debts for the year ended 31 March 20X5

(c) Drag and drop the account names to the debit and credit columns to show where the entries for the journal would be made.

(3 marks)

Debit
Drawings

Credit
Purchases

Goods held for resale by the business were taken by the owner for her own personal use. No postings have been made.

If goods (purchases) were taken out of the business for the owner's personal use the double entry is **DR Drawings and CR Purchases** for the cost of the goods taken personally by the owner. Drawings increase for the owner and expenses (purchases) are decreased by the business cost of the goods taken.

Task 5 (20 marks)

Part (a) 6 marks

This task can examine adjustments to a sales ledger control account (SLCA), purchase ledger control account (PLCA) or the cash book from reconciliations already undertaken in the task.

Account	Dr £	Cr £
Item 2		246
Item 5	180	
Item 6	4500	

The balance showing on the bank statement is a debit of £3,285 and the balance in the cash book is a credit of £7,033. Therefore, both indicate the bank balance is overdrawn.

1.	A BACS payment to a supplier for the month of December 20X3 for £600 had not yet cleared the bank statements. **A timing difference does not affect the cash book but would be required to reconcile the cash book to the closing balance as per the bank statement.**
2.	Interest paid of £246 showing in the bank statements for the month of December 20X3 were not been entered in the cash book. **The omitted item must be credited to the cash book as a payment. CR Cash Book £246.**
3.	A remittance advice from a customer has been received and an entry made in the cash book for the correct amount of £1,040. This is not yet showing on the bank statements. **A timing difference which does not affect the cash book but would be required to reconcile the cash book to the closing balance as per the bank statement.**
4.	The bank has made an error. Interest paid of £246 for the month of December 20X3 has been in error debited twice on the bank statements. **Debited on a bank statement means payment has been taken twice by the bank. The bank error does not affect the cash book but is an adjustment required to reconcile the cash book to the closing balance as per the bank statement.**
5.	A faster payment of £3,460 has been recorded in the cash book in error as £3,640. **A payment from the cash book would be a credit entry and £3,640 has been credited. It should have been a credit of £3,460. So, £180 too much has been credited to the cash book. We will need to debit the cash book (£3,640 - £3,460) to reduce the £180 overpayment recorded. DR Cash Book £180.**
6.	A BACS receipt from a customer for £4,500 appears on the bank statements but was not recorded in the cash book. **The omitted item needs to be recorded as a receipt in the cash book. DR Cash Book £4,500.**

A cash book showing the adjustments and the bank reconciliation (agreement) has been shown below to aid logic and further understanding.

Bank

	£		£
Item 5	180	Balance b/d	7033
Item 6	4500	Item 2	246
Balance c/d	2599		
	7279		7279

Bank reconciliation

	£
Balance as per bank statement	-3285
Item 1	-600
Item 3	1040
Item 4	246
Revised (corrected) cash book balance	-2599

Part (b) 3 marks

(b) Drag and drop the account names to the debit and credit columns to show where the entries for total payroll costs for an accounting period should be made.

Debit
Wages expense

Credit
Wages control

Total payroll costs (wages) should be debited to expenses (to increase expenses) and credited to a wages control account (increasing a liability) and representing wages owed until paid.

Part (c) 11 marks

(c) Extend the figures into the columns for the statement of profit or loss and the statement of financial position. Do NOT enter zeros into unused column cells. Complete the extended trial balance by totalling the columns and entering any profit or loss figure for the year ended.

(11 marks)

Tutor note: the trial balance has two adjustments for closing inventory. The DR (an asset) for closing inventory to be included in the statement of financial position and a CR (reduction to purchases expenses) for closing inventory to be included within the statement of profit or loss for the year ended.

The exam will have autosum function for the trial balance totals, so you will not need to add up your columns in the exam task. There is also a picklist selection for the profit or loss for the year end which when the amount is included it should balance the last 4 columns of the ETB. If a profit for example below, then the profit amount is a debit to the statement of profit or loss (closing the profit or loss account for the year) and a credit (transfer) to the statement of financial position (increasing the capital account balance owed to the owner of the business).

Ledger account	Ledger balances		Adjustments		Statement of profit or loss		Statement of financial position	
	Dr £	Cr £	Dr £	Cr £	Dr £	Cr £	Dr £	Cr £
Bank overdraft		8099		1400				9499
Fixtures and fittings at cost	40000						40000	
Fixtures and fittings accumulated depreciation		8000		4000				12000
Purchases	44322				44322			
Purchase ledger control account		4398		88				4486
Sales		87000				87000		
Sales ledger control account	5000						5000	
Rent expenses	10000		2000		12000			
Staff wages	5040			2000	3040			
Light and heat	2391				2391			
Depreciation charges			4000		4000			
VAT		4724	1545					3179
Miscellaneous expenses	449				449			
Opening inventory	1300				1300			
Accruals				2000				2000
Capital		14338						14338
Closing inventory			2322	2322		2322	2322	
Drawings	18000		2000				20000	
Suspense	57		1488	1545				
Profit/loss for the year					21820			21820
Total	126559	126559	13355	13355	89322	89322	67322	67322